Schwebel

"They travelled
Through the
Wilderness"

Exodus 15:22 They traveled through the wilderness...
26 x 19 in   etching and graphite   1997

SCHWEBEL

DAVID'S JOURNEY

FROM THE BOOKS OF SAMUEL AND KINGS

INTRODUCTION BY EVERETT FOX

A STABILIZED CHAOS PUBLICATION   JERUSALEM

YESHIVA UNIVERSITY MUSEUM   NEW YORK

This edition was published on the occasion of the inaugural
exhibition of the Yeshiva University Museum at the Center
for Jewish History, 15 West 16ᵗʰ Street, New York City.
June - December, 2000.

It is composed of *David, The King*, published in Israel in
1998, and preceded by a 48 page supplement of more recent
paintings to be exhibited at the museum. This supplement was
made possible by a grant from the New York - Israel Cultural
Cooperation Commission and the Consulate General of Israel
in New York, Office of Cultural Affairs.

A Stabilized Chaos Publication
P.O.B. 3595, Jerusalem 91035, Israel

Photography and Production: The Jerusalem Photograph Studio
Plates and color separations: Tafsar L. Ltd., Jerusalem
Printed by Z.Z. Print Ltd., Tel Aviv

To my wife, Adva Frank Schwebel.

ACKNOWLEDGEMENTS

The production of this edition could not have taken place without the help of Michael Amar of the Jerusalem Photographic Studio and the expertise of Tafsar Ltd.

The design and mounting of the exhibition at the Yeshiva University Museum was expertly done by Kenneth Segal. Daniel Marom, whose writing appears in this edition, has always made his knowledge of Jewish history available to me.

Everett Fox is a particular genius in knowledge of the Bible. I am fortunate to have his introduction here and to have him use my work to illuminate his.

This exhibition was made possible by the unwavering support of Sylvia Herskowitz, Director of the Yeshiva University Museum.

I wish to thank the Jewish Publication Society for permitting me to use their translations of the Bible, and Schocken Books for allowing Everett Fox's translation and writings to play a vital part in this book-catalogue.

This publication was generously supported by the following grants:
The Rich Foundation, Tel Aviv.
The New York-Israel Cultural Commission and the Consulate General
of Israel in New York, Office of Cultural Affairs.
The Israelow Family Circle, in memory of Uncle Paul.

Schwebel

P.O.Box 3595, Jerusalem, 91035, Israel

Contents of the Supplement to *David, The King*

Contents of *David, The King*

On a Bronx Street
44 x 52 in.   2000

II Samuel 22: 3,4 David's last words:
A ruler over humans, a righteous one,
a ruler with the awe of God,
is like the light of daybreak as the sun rises,
a daybreak without clouds,
by dint of brightness,
by dint of rain, the herbage of earth.

Preface

Schwebel has referred to himself as a receiving vessel, a phrase which Martin Buber used to describe the way that a man of today should confront the Bible - without any preconceived notions. This is exactly how I first met the artist himself. It was summer and my office was relatively quiet. I had fallen into that pleasant state of relaxation that comes when the desk is uncluttered and the air conditioner works fine.

Schwebel was a surprise. He was wearing shorts and a T-shirt with a bandana around his neck. He walked in jauntily, confidently - certainly not your typical Israeli artist visiting New York. It turned out that he is an American, born in West Virginia and raised in the Bronx, a point I have heard him make often, always with pleasure.

That afternoon, Schwebel was anything but a receiving vessel. I was jolted out of my summer torpor by his confrontational manner. He reminded me, I told him, of Gully Jimson in *The Horse's Mouth*, to which he immediately responded with a quote from the book: "I like to keep my pictures above dog level." When he left, we parted on very amicable terms. He kissed me on the cheek and gave me a copy of his book *David, The King*, which he inscribed "for Herskowitz, a 'victim of my own success.'"

It was a couple of days before I had a chance to go through the book, and when I did, I was blown away. Such power in the painting, such confidence in the drawing. Rage and tenderness, anguish and desire, exploding on the canvas in crimsons and corals, now slashed and jagged, now polished and silky - and almost always behind the explosive figures the superbly drawn familiar streets of Jerusalem. I turned the pages quickly without reading the text: Saul, David, Jonathan, Bathsheba, Uriah - they all were there, summoned by the artist's passionate ferocity, raised from the dead to reenact in post modern times their triumphs and their desolation. When I started reading the narrative, the artist's notes interwoven with quotations from the Bible, Buber, Bialik, Primo Levi...I realized that the triumphs and desolation were also Schwebel's, the angst with which he has wrestled, like *Yaakov Avinu*, our forefather Jacob, all his life. By restaging the biblical drama in his own time, Schwebel confronts his own personal, familial, and social demons.

Surely this was the artist whose work would open our new museum at the Center for Jewish History. What could be a more appropriate theme than David himself, precursor of the Messiah, the most revered and creative of all Jewish heroes?

I met with Schwebel many times since that summer day. We became good friends who trust each other. It was in a coffee shop in Jerusalem that he mentioned bringing David to New York, not just the show, but his iconic presence. Schwebel attacked this idea with great gusto, and within a few months there arrived photos of David spotting Bathsheba on a roof over Canal Street, or whirling with the Ark on the Williamsburg Bridge, or fighting Goliath on 42nd Street - clearly exultant paintings.

In attempting to define the nature of Schwebel's emotional arsenal, why his paintings pack such a wallop, I suddenly thought of a Hamlet in modern dress directed by John Gielgud and another, the Joseph Papp rock musical, which shocked the world in 1968. Both Gielgud and Papp wanted the audience to discover the veins of the living original, buried under accumulated layers of reverential varnish. The conflation that both productions exploited heightened their audience's perception and, in one critic's words, sent "shafts of intense light on over-familiar passages."

This is what Schwebel's paintings offer us—shafts of intense light on over-familiar texts.

Sylvia Axelrod Herskowitz
February, 2000

The Painter's Introduction

These paintings, drawings and etchings follow the story of David as told in the book of Samuel and continued in the beginning of Kings where the end of his life is described. For almost twenty years these works have been my response to the wars and threats of wars in Israel, to political intrigues, including murder, and religious conflicts within – and to the excitement of the land. I cannot help but explore the streets of New York for this purpose in the realization that the Bible travels and the situations David and others are placed in are an incredible match for today. I have used them as such, transferring the seasonings of my own life into David or Saul and even Tamar.

Therefore, there are no period costumes and no symbols. I use anyone to model for the actors: baseball pitchers from the past give Shimei authenticity when he throws stones at David. I reinterpret Caravaggio's young lute player as David when he entertains King Saul and my mirror image yields the jealousy and madness of the aging King. Katherine Hepburn portrays Bat-Sheva's last years and without clothes she's from Muybridge's photographs taken in the 1870's. Ingrid Bergman is fine for the young beauty Abishag presented to David so that "he will be warm".

Martin Buber's remarks reprinted here explain how one might arrive at such an approach. His ideas seem to support the severe propositions I often end up with, such as King Saul's attempt on David's life outside my studio in Judea, or the prophet Samuel hearing God's admonitions near a subway entrance on 23rd Street, or David whirling with the Ark in the market of Jerusalem or on the Williamsburg Bridge…and even into the Holocaust. (Certainly a renaissance painter wouldn't think twice about using his courtyard as a setting for the Passion of Christ.)

These works are executed in combinations of drawing and paint, usually graphite and oils. The city streets are drawn in graphite to make them recognizable and enhance the drama of the situation. Color might ignite my imagination prematurely and transform the often nondescript Jaffa Road into Broadway, or the near monumental plastic roofing of the Mahane Yehuda Market into a Gothic church. I draw just enough detail before allowing graphite and color to shake free and begin to play, knowing that my color is at its best when held responsive to the graphite.

Two dates are often listed for the paintings because I have grown very fond of recycling earlier works, reworking them for new tasks. I re-enter any period of my life when the need arises, raging through my storerooms to confiscate those paintings that might have other uses, saving needed parts to juxtapose against a new plot. A high speed disc-sander eliminates the rest. (The first painting in this book, *"a daybreak without clouds, by dint of brightness, by dint of rain, the herbage of the earth"*, was recycled from a 1981 Bronx street painting, eliminating in the process the original "three sewer stickball hero", but on page S33 he remains as a witness.)

The Hebrew version of this book, entitled *David*, was published in 1997. An English edition appeared a year later with several additions. This volume expands upon both because the Bible constantly offers new discoveries and has influenced me to create different versions of the same subject or add new episodes. Now Samuel hears God's voice near a subway entrance on 23rd Street, and the George Washington Bridge is the backdrop when Tamar exits after being raped; Saul hunts for David on the 14th Street subway platform and Bat-Sheva bathes on a roof over Canal Street – my New York heritage mixing with my thirty-seven years in Israel.

As for the translation into English, Everett Fox, in his preface to his translation of the *Five Books of Moses*, Schocken Books, 1995, states that he "is guided by the principle that the Hebrew Bible, like much of the literature of antiquity, was meant to be read aloud, and that consequently it must be translated with careful attention to rhythm and sound" and that "such an approach was first espoused by Martin Buber and Franz Rosenzweig in their monumental German translation of the Bible". I have structured the excerpts from the books of Samuel and Kings after this principle, except where Fox has already done so in his translation. I tried to make this book as uncluttered as possible to retain the power of the Bible. I hope that I have become, in Buber's words, a "receiving vessel."

These are the six translations I use, selected for their clarity or poetic value:
[1] *The Tanakh*, Jewish Publication Society, 1985. This appears most frequently.
[2] The Society's 1917 translation as it appears in the Soncino Press editions of
Samuel (1949) and Kings (1950).
[3] The Holy Bible, New International Version, 1978.
[4] The Holy Bible, King James Version.
[5] The early translation of II Samuel 11-12, the entire David and Bat-Sheva episode by Everett Fox "intended to echo the Hebrew, and to lead the reader back to the sound structure and form of the original."
[6] The final translation by Everett Fox of The Book of Samuel, *Give Us A King!,* Schocken Books, 1999. I regret being unable to utilize this new version for all the biblical passages in my book.

The name of the publisher of this book, A Stabilized Chaos Publication, is derived from Bernard Berenson's definition of art – the artist's task is to stabilize chaos.

I do not imagine that you will expect me to give you any so-called character sketches of biblical leaders. That would be an impossible undertaking, for the Bible does not concern itself with character nor with individuality, and one cannot draw from it any description of character or individualities. The Bible depicts something else, namely, persons in situations. The Bible is not concerned with the difference between these persons; but the difference between the situations in which the person, the creaturely person, the appointed person, stands his test or fails, is all-important to it.

Martin Buber, "On The Bible", from *The Man of Today and the Jewish Bible,* N.Y., Schocken Books.

Schwebel's David

Everett Fox

As a translator and commentator, it has been my experience that the human face of the Hebrew Bible is at once distant and unerringly close. Rarely does an entire life journey unfold in the biblical text; more often than not, we are given something akin to scenes from a play, moments of great drama which define the essence of a human life as response to the divine command.

This is especially true of the Bible's central human figure, David, who occupies even more space in its pages than Moses itself. Despite our centuries-long attraction to David – his name means "beloved" – we search the text in vain to uncover his inner life. Just when we feel we are about to see into his heart, mirrored in Saul's jealousy, Jonathan's deep friendship, his wives' love, or his subordinates' violent loyalty, David pulls away, hiding his true feelings, and we are left with a story in which the concept of Israelite monarchy, as a threat to divine kingship, looks as if it might overwhelm the full portrayal of character.

But the Bible's great strength, and the secret of its enduring power, lies in its ability to present the human dilemmas of its characters with terrible intensity, at the same time that it sets forth divine demands. For me, that intensity was something I sensed in the text as I progressed in my translation work, but which was decisively brought home to me through the medium of Schwebel's great encounter with the David story.

In Schwebel's work, unlike most of the Bible illustrations of the Middle Ages, God is invisible, rather it is the utterly human situations which cry out in every painting, every drawing, every etching. And what situations they are! The political agony of the theocratic Samuel, the madness of Saul, pushed over the brink by his failure to lead, the furtiveness, first, and later the great life-fullness of David, which must eventually give way to despair and decline. And this is not to mention the struggles of supporting characters, from Bat-Sheva to Tamar to Avsalom.

Schwebel has well understood Martin Buber's admonition (which he quotes) to "yield to [the Bible], withhold nothing of its being, and let whatever will occur between himself and it." His art is a literally graphic example of such a meeting, an encounter unaffected by the dense layers of scholarship and tradition which so often enrich and so often stultify. Schwebel's work on David is mediated only by his own life experience and by his encounter with the landscape of New York, Jerusalem and Judea. But it rings deeply true to the pathos of the Samuel and Kings narratives. Even what may appear to be a whim – for example his portrayal of the rock-throwing Shimei of II Samuel 20 in the garb of early twentieth century baseball pitchers – is but the powerful internalization of the biblical text through the medium of another world.

I know of no other artist who has expended so much concentrated effort – almost two decades and an output of several hundred pieces – on one extended story, biblical or otherwise, especially outside the parameters of book illustration. Several scenes, to be sure, repeat numerous times: the victory over Goliath (I Sam.17), David whirling before God (II Sam.6), David seeing Bat-Sheva (II Sam.11), David arising from the earth (II Sam.12), Tamar after the rape (II Sam. 13), Shimei pelting David (II Sam.16), the king sitting at the gateway (II Sam. 18). What unifies these repeated works thematically is their focus on dramatic emotional moments; but what is often characteristic of them visually is a pervading sense of physical motion. Even in scenes whose subject is a standing or sitting or reclining figure, there is an unrelentingly restless sense of movement, if not in the human subject then in the accompanying figures, the architectural background, or the natural setting. Unlike the West's most famous artistic representation of David, the matchless Michelangelo sculpture whose young hero is the epitome of classical perfection in repose, Schwebel's David is a man perpetually in motion. Even when he sits before God (in the text, as he is about to ask the deity for permission to build a Temple), he is not at peace, in thoughtful prayer, but in a tense pose of clenched fists (Schwebel's works on this theme were painted shortly after the Rabin assassination, and reveal more anger and pain than meditation). Similarly, the paintings that show old David asleep, another repeated scene, do not portray the sleep of the satiated, but rather a final moment of exhaustion, a futile attempt to rest by an old man whose life has made it impossible for him to know peace. Above all is the scene that appears in Schwebel's David *oeuvre* more than any other: the whirling king, rejoicing at the bringing of the Ark to Jerusalem. Here David becomes a biblical Zorba, dancing the dance of life despite the burdens of his office, his impending disastrous future, the modern-day traffic of Jerusalem, and even, incongruously breaking into Schwebel's imagery, Auschwitz itself.

The dancing of David, of course, resembles the artist closely, and that is neither accident nor frivolity. Only one who has absorbed the biblical narrative in his or her bones can reproduce or perform it, as it were. Schwebel might describe himself as being seduced or even ambushed by the David stories; but whatever the process was, he has in fact been seized by them (a prophetic metaphor) and has transferred that experience to canvas and paper for all to see. In this he has hearkened back to the consciousness of medieval readers, Jewish and Christian, for whom the Bible, imbibed in their mother's milk, was the great text to which their lives were merely commentary.

So dance David's dance with Schwebel. You will discover, whether out on Canal Street or hiding in the pots and pans of Mahane Yehuda, the Bible's enduring power to evoke the human drama in the ancient warrior-poet king from Bethlehem. And you will thus find in Schwebel's work a great act of translation.

The Man of Today

The man of today has no access to a sure and solid faith, nor can it be made accessible to him. If he examines himself seriously, he knows this and may not delude himself further. But he is not denied the possibility of holding himself open to faith. If he is really serious, he too can open up this book and let its rays strike him where they will. He can give himself up and submit to the test without preconceived notions and without reservations. He can absorb the Bible with all his strength, and wait to see what will happen to him, whether he will not discover within himself a new and unbiased approach to this or that element in the book. But to this end, he must read the Jewish Bible as though it were something entirely unfamiliar, as though it had not been set before him ready-made, at school and after in the light of "religious" and "scientific" certainties; as though he has not been confronted all his life with sham concepts and sham statements which cited the Bible as their authority. He must face the book with a new attitude as something new. He must yield to it, withhold nothing of his being, and let whatever will occur between himself and it. He does not know which of its sayings and images will overwhelm him and mould him, from where the spirit will ferment and enter into him, to incorporate itself anew in his body. But he holds himself open. He does not believe anything a priori; he does not disbelieve anything a priori. He reads aloud the words written in the book in front of him; he hears the words he utters and it reaches him. Nothing is prejudged. The current of time flows on, and the contemporary character of this man becomes itself a receiving vessel.

Martin Buber, "The Man of Today and the Jewish Bible", Schocken Books, 1948,1963. From a series of lectures delivered in Berlin, 1926.

"David was whirling with all his might" / the Williamsburg Bridge, Delancy Street below
44 x 50 in   1999
(see page 62)

I Samuel 8: 4-22

So all the elders of Israel gathered together and came to Shemu'el at Rama,
they said to him: Here, you have grown old,
and your sons do not walk in your ways.
So-now, make us a king
to lead-us-as-judge, like all the other nations!
Now the manner was evil in the eyes of Shemu'el, when they said:
Give us a king, to lead-us-as-judge!
So Shemu'el prayed to YHWH,
and YHWH said to Shemu'el:
Hearken to the voice of the people
in all that they say to you;
indeed, it is not you whom they have rejected,
indeed it is I whom they have rejected from being-king over them,
in accordance with all the doings that they have done
from the day I brought them up from Egypt until this day:
they have abandoned me, serving other gods!
Thus they are doing to you as well!
So-now, hearken to their voice;
however: indeed, you are to warn, yes, warn them,
by telling them the practice of the king who will reign-as king over them.
Shemu'el said all the words of YHWH
to the people who were requesting from him a king, he said:
This will be the practice of the king who will reign-as-king over you:
Your sons he will take away,
setting him in his chariots and among his riders,
so that they will run ahead of his chariot;
to make them commanders of thousands and commanders of fifties,
to plow his plowing and harvest his harvest,
and to make his battle weapons and his chariot weapons;
your daughters he will take-away as ointment mixers, as cooks, and as bakers;
your fields, your vineyards, and your olive groves, the best-ones,
he will take-away and give to his servants;
your sowing seed and your vine-fruit he will tithe
and give to his officers and to his servants;
your servants, your maids, and your young men, the best ones,
and your donkeys, he will take away, that they may do his work;
your flock he will tithe, and you yourselves will be for him as slaves.
And you will cry out on that day
because of your king whom you have chosen for yourselves,
but YHWH will not answer you on that day!
But the people refused to hearken to Shemu'el's voice,
They said: No! Rather, let there be a king over us
so that we, we too may be like all the other nations!
When Shemu'el heard all the people's words,
He spoke them in the ears of YHWH.
And YHWH said to Shemu'el:
Hearken to their voice: you are to king them a king!
Shemu'el said to the men of Israel: Go, each-man to his town!

[6]

"Give us a king" / neo-classic architecture over a Judean hill
(After a photograph by Robert Capa of new immigrants to Israel.)

63 x 59 in   1999

"Give us a king" / Broadway apartment building over a Judean hill with
            Israeli political demonstrators

63 x 59 in   1999

"Give us a king"   /   Judea with a lower Broadway monumental building.
                         (The group is drawn after Robert Capa's 1948
                         photograph of an election meeting in Tel Aviv)
39 x 51 in.   1979, 1995

I Samuel 16: 1-5

YHWH said to Shemu'el:

How long will you keep-on-mourning for Sha'ul,

when I myself have rejected him from being king over Israel?

Fill your horn with oil and go.

I am sending you to Yishai the Betlehemite,

for I have selected a king for me from among his sons.

Shemu'el said:

How can I go?

If Sha'ul hears, he will kill me!

YHWH said:

A she-calf of the herd you are to take in your hand;

you are to say:

It is to slaughter-offer to YHWH that I have come.

Then you are to call Yishai for the slaughter-meal,

and I myself will make-known to you what you are to do;

you are to anoint for me the one that I tell you to.

Shemu'el did that which YHWH had spoken,

he came to Bet Lehem,

and the elders of the town trembled to meet him,

they said:

Is it in peace, your coming?

He said:

In peace—

it is to slaughter-offer to YHWH that I have come!

Purify-yourselves

so that you may come with me to the slaughter-meal.

So he purified Yishai and his sons

and called them to the slaughter-meal.

[6]

" YHWH said to Samuel: How long will you keep on mourning for Saul…?"
23rd Street and 7th Avenue, N.Y.C.
56 x 53 in   1999

I Samuel 17: 41-49

And the Philistine went-along, going and coming-nearer to David,
with the man, the shield bearer, before him.
And when the Philistine looked and saw David, he taunted him,
for he was only a lad,
and ruddy, fair to look at.
The Philistine said to David:
Am I a dog,
that you come at me with sticks?
And the Philistine cursed David by his gods.
The Philistine said to David:
Come to me,
that I may give your flesh to the fowl of the heavens
    and to the beasts of the field!
But David said to the Philistine:
You come to me
with a sword and a scimitar and a spear,
but I come to you
with the name of YHWH of the Heavenly-Armies,
the God of the ranks of Israel, whom you have mocked!
This day, YHWH will turn you over to my hand,
so that I will strike-you-down
and will remove your head from you;
I will give your carcass and the carcass of the Philistine camp
    this day
to the fowl of the heavens and to the wildlife of the earth,
so that all the earth may know that Israel has a God,
and that all this assembly may know
that it is not with a sword or with a spear that YHWH delivers –
for the battle is YHWH's,
and he will give all of you into our hand!
And it was, when the Philistine arose to come-near to meet David,
that David hurried-out and ran toward the ranks to meet the Philistine:
and David stretched out his hand to the bag,
he took from there a stone, and slung it,
    and he struck the Philistine on his forehead:
the stone sank into his forehead
and he fell on his face to the ground.

[6]

This was originally commissioned by the owner of the Art deco
landmark building next to the bus terminal, that is, before David's
appearance. The metallic green and brass elements in the lobby
substitute for the extensive reconstruction presently going on elsewhere
on 42nd Street. Goliath is on the north side, close to 7th Avenue, while
David hurls from the street itself. (Fox's spelling within his translation
is always attune to actual Hebrew pronunciation: Goliath becomes Golyat,
Shaul is Sha'ul, and Samuel is Shemu'el)

David and Goliath   /   42nd Street, New York
64 x 51 in   1999

I Samuel 18: 5-10
And David went out,
and everywhere that Sha'ul sent him, he prospered.
Sha'ul placed him over the men of war,
and it was good in the eyes of all the people,
    and also in the eyes of Sha'ul's servants.
And it was in their coming-back, at David's return from striking the Philistine,
that women went out from all the towns in Israel, for singing and dances,
to meet King Sha'ul with timbrels, with joyful sounds and with triangles.
And the dancing women chanted and said:
    Sha'ul has struck-down his thousands,
    But David—his myriads!
Sha'ul became exceedingly upset,
this matter was evil in his eyes,
he said to himself:
They give-credit to David for myriads,
but to me they give credit for thousands!
There yet remains for him only the kingdom!
And Sha'ul was keeping-an-eye on David from that day on.

Now it was on the morrow,
that an evil spirit of God surged upon Sha'ul, and he ranted-
    like-a-prophet in the midst of the house,
while David was playing the lyre with his hand,
    as he had day after day,
and there was a spear in Sha'ul's hand;
                    [6]

David plays for Saul
52 x 44 in   1999

David is painted after a head of a young man
by the Italian sculptor Nicolas Pisano, circa 1300.
The aging king's two moods are after myself.

I Samuel 23: 25-26
Then Sha'ul and his men went to seek for him,
when it was told to David,
he went down to a certain crag and stayed in the Wilderness of Ma'on.
When Sha'ul heard, he pursued after David, in the wilderness of Ma'on.
And Sha'ul went on one side of a hill, over-here,
with David and his men on the other side of the hill, over-there,
And David was in haste to get away from Sha'ul,
while Sha'ul and his men were closing in on David...

[6]

King Saul hunts David / 14th Street subway platform
45 ½ x 56 in 1999

I Samuel 24: 1-16

Now it was, when Sha'ul returned from pursuing after the Philistines,
that it was told to him, saying:
Here, David is in the Wilderness of Ein Gedi!
So Sha'ul took three thousand men, hand-picked from all Israel,
and went to seek out David and his men, in front of the Wild-Goat Rocks.
He came to some sheep pens along the way, and there was a cave there;
and Sha'ul went in to "cover his feet,"
while David and his men were staying in the recesses of the cave.
David's men said to him: Here is the day about which YHWH said to you:
Here, I give your enemy into your hand!
You may do with him whatever seems-good in your eyes!
So David arose and cut off the corner of the cloak that belonged to Sha'ul, stealthily.
But it was after that, that David's heart struck him with remorse,
because he had cut off the corner that belonged to Sha'ul,
He said to his men: Heaven forbid for me from YHWH
if I should do this thing to my lord, to YHWH's anointed,
to stretch out my hand against him, for he is YHWH's anointed!
And David rebuked his men with these words,
And did not give-them-leave to rise up against Sha'ul,
while Sha'ul arose from the cave, and went on his way.
But David arose after that
and came-out of the cave, and he called out after Sha'ul saying:
My lord king!
When Sha'ul looked behind him,
David bowed, brow to the ground, and prostrated-himself,
and David said to Sha'ul: Why do you hearken to people's words who are saying:
Here, David is seeking evil-against-you?
Here, this day your own eyes have seen
how YHWH gave you today into my hand, in this cave;
I intended to kill you, but I had compassion on you:
I said to myself: I will not stretch out my hand against my lord,
for he is YHWH's anointed!
And father, see too: see the corner of your cloak in my hand—
for when I cut off the corner of your cloak, I did not kill you!
So learn and see that there is no evil or rebellion in my hand,
nor have I sinned against you—
yet you are stalking my life, to take it!
May YHWH see justice-done between me and you—
And may YHWH take-vengeance for me upon you—
But my hand shall not be against you!
As the ancient proverb says: from wicked ones comes wickedness!
but my hand shall not be against you!
After whom has the king of Israel gone out? After whom are you pursuing?
After a dead dog? After a single flea?
May YHWH be decider, and may he judge between me and you:
when he sees, may he uphold my cause
and exact-justice from your hand!

[6]

(see page 50 for the story about David and the spider)

David cuts off the corner of Shemu'el's cloak / Judean hillside
63 x 59 in   1999

I Samuel 28: 7-16

So Sha'ul said to his servants: Seek for me a woman, a possessor of ghosts,
that I may go to her, that I may consult the dead through her.
His servants said to him: Here, there is a woman, a possessor of ghosts, at EnDor.
Sha'ul disguised himself, clothing himself in other garments,
and then he went, he and two men with him,
and came to the woman at night.
He said: Pray divine for me by a ghost,
bring-up for me the one that I will say to you!
The woman said to him: Here, you know what Sha'ul has done,
how he has cut off ghosts and favorable-spirits from the land.
So why do you want to ensnare my life, to cause-my-death?
So Sha'ul swore to her by YHWH, saying:
As YHWH lives, should any guilt befall you through this matter…!
The woman said: Whom should I bring-up for you?
He said: Bring-up Shemu'el for me.
Now when the woman saw Shemu'el,
she cried out in a loud voice,
the woman said to Sha'ul, saying:
Why have you deceived me?
You are Sha'ul!
The king said to her: Don't be afraid;
rather, what do you see?
The woman said to Sha'ul:
I see a god-like being coming up from the ground.
He said to her: What is its form?
She said: An old man is coming up,
and he is wrapped in a cloak.
Then Sha'ul knew that it was Shemu'el,
and he bowed, brow to the ground, and prostrated himself.
Shemu'el said to Sha'ul:
Why have you disturbed me, by bringing me up?
Sha'ul said: I am exceedingly distressed—
the Philistines are waging battle against me,
and God has turned away from me:
he no longer answers me,
either by the hand of the prophets or by dreams.
So I have called you to make-known to me what I should do!
Shemu'el said: Why do you make-request of me?
For YHWH has turned away from you and has gone-over to your fellow!
YHWH has done to you as he promised by my hand:
YHWH has torn away the kingdom from your hand
and has given it to your fellow, to David…

[6]

Excerpt from Fox's introduction to *Give Us A King*!: Despite Saul's failures and his
subsequent descent into monomaniacal pursuit of David, there is something that leads
many readers to view the first king of Israel not as evil, but as tragically marred. The
final stories about him, at En Dor and in battle at Mt. Gilboa [see p.55], naturally elicit
sympathy…

The Ghost at En Dor / Southern entrance to Central Park, New York
52 ½ x 43   2000

David Whirls / The Deportation Train mounted on Jerome Avenue subway tracks
22 x 29 ½ in   1994
(Further work on this subject can be seen on pages 74-79)

"David whirling with all his might" / Deportation Train and the Bronx stick-ball hero
50 x 56 in   1981, 2000

II Samuel 11: 1-5
Now it was at the turning of the year, at the time of kings' going forth,
that David sent Yo'av and his servants with him, and all Israel:
they wrought-ruin to the Children of Amnon and besieged Rabba,
while David stayed in Jerusalem.
Now it was around the time of sunset
that David arose from his lying-place and went-for-a-walk
　　upon the roof of the king's house,
and he saw a woman washing herself, from on the roof,
the woman was exceedingly fair to look at.
David sent and asked after the woman:
they said: Isn't this Bat-Sheva daughter of Eli'am, wife of Uriyya the Hittite?
David sent messengers, and he had-her-brought,
she came to him and he lay with her
--now she had just purified-herself from her state of *tum'a--,*
then she returned to her house.
The woman became pregnant,
she sent and had-it-told to David, she said: I am pregnant!
[6]

From Fox's introduction to *Give Us A King!:* As ruler of a small empire, as a
military and political success, David seems to be the king with everything,
including multiple wives and sons to succeed him. Into this moment of triumph,
the Bible inserts the turning point of II Samuel and one of the greatest of all
biblical tales: the story of David and Bat-Sheva. While later Jewish tradition,
both in the biblical book of Chronicles (which omits the story) and in the
Talmud (which whitewashes David), clearly found it difficult to reconcile the
important symbolic figure of David with the way he appears in this story, the
Book of Samuel features it dramatically as the root of much that is to follow,
and lavishes a good deal of artistic attention and skill upon it.

David and Bat-Sheva / Canal Street, New York
59 x 53 in   1999

II Samuel 11: 6-11
So David sent word to Yo'av:
Send me Uriyyah the Hittite.
And Yo'av sent Uriyyah to David.
When Uriyyah came to him,
David inquired after the well-being of Yo'av, the well-being of
    the fighting-people, and the well-being of the battle,
then David said to Uriyyah:
Go-down to your house and wash your feet!
Uriyyah went out of the king's house,
and after him went out a portion from the king,
but Uriyyah lay down at the entrance to the king's house,
    with all his lord's servants,
he did not go-down to his house.
They told David, saying:
Uriyyah has not gone-down to his house.
David said to Uriyyah:
Isn't it from a long journey that you have come?
Why haven't you gone down to your house?
Uriyyah said to David:
The Coffer and Israel and Judah are staying at Sukkot,
my lord Yo'av and my lord's servants are camping on
the surface of the open-field—
and I, I should come into my house
to eat and to drink and to lie with my wife?
As you live, as your very being lives: Were I to do this thing…!

                                          [6]

(for further works on this subject, see page 100)

David and Uriyyah / Canal Street roof, New York
40 x 60 in   1999

II Samuel 13:1-10
Avsalom son of David had a fair sister, her name was Tamar,
and Amnon son-of-David fell in love with her.
And Amnon was distressed to the point of making himself-sick
   because of Tamar his sister,
for she was a virgin,
and so it seemed-impossible in Amnon's eyes to do anything to her.
Amnon had a friend, his name was Yonadav son of Shim'a,
   David's brother;
and Yonadav was a exceedingly worldly-wise man.
He said to him:
Why are you so haggard, O son of the king, morning after morning?
Shouldn't you tell me?
Amnon said to him:
It's Tamar, sister of Avsalom my brother—I love her!
Yonadad said to him:
Lie down on your lying-place and feign-sickness;
when your father comes to see you, say to him:
Pray let Tamar my sister come and feed me some bread,
let her make-ready some food before my eyes,
   in order that I may see,
and I will eat from her hand.

So Amnon lay-down and feigned-sickness,
and when the king came to see him, Amnon said to the king:
Pray let Tamar my sister come
and heat two heart-shaped-dumplings before my eyes,
that I may be-fed from her own hand.
David sent word to Tamar, in the palace-house, saying:
Pray go to the house of Amnon your brother,
and make-ready for him some food.
So Tamar went to the house of Amnon her brother,
    while he was lying down.
She took some dough, kneaded it, heated it before his eyes
and boiled the heart-shaped dumplings,
then she took the pot and placed it before him,
but he refused to eat.
Amnon said: Have everyone go out from me!
And everyone went out from him.
Amnon said to Tamar:
Bring the food into the inner-room,
    that I may be-fed from your own hand.
So Tamar took the heart-shaped dumplings she had made,
and brought them to Amnon her brother, into the inner room.

[6]

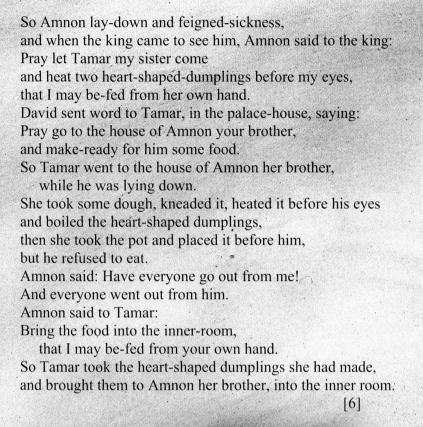

II Samuel 13: 11-21
When she brought them close to him for him to eat,
he overpowered her and said to her:
Come, lie with me, sister!
She said to him:
No, brother, do *not* force me,
for such is not to be done in Israel—
don't do the vile-thing!
And as for me, where would I take my disgrace?
And as for you, you would be like one of the vile-ones in Israel!
So-now, pray speak to the king—he will not withhold me from you.
But he would not hearken to her voice,
he overpowered her and forced her, lying with her.
And then Amnon hated her with an exceedingly great hatred,
indeed, greater was the hatred with which he hated her
than the love with which he had loved her;
Amnon said to her: Get-up, go-away!
She said to him:
About this great evil—more than the other-thing that you did
    to me—sending me away…!
But he would not hearken to her;
he called to his attending lad
and said: Pray send this-one away from me, outside,
and locked the door behind her!
--Now on her was an ornamental tunic,
for thus were clothed the king's virgin daughters in robes.--
So his attendant brought her outside, and locked the door behind her.
And Tamar put ashes onto her head,
while the ornamented tunic that was on her, she tore;
she put her hands on her head
and went-along, going-along and crying out.
Avsalom her brother said to her:
Has Amnon your brother been with you?
Now, sister, be silent—he is your brother;
don't take this thing to heart!
So Tamar sat desolate in the house of Avsalom her brother.
Now King David heard about all these things,
and he was exceedingly upset.
And Avsalom did not speak with Amnon,
    anything from evil to good.
For Avsalom hated Amnon over the fact that he had forced
    Tamar his sister.

[6]

(Avsalom eventually has Amnon killed)

The rape of Tamar: "And Tamar put ashes onto her head" / George Washington Bridge
48 x 38 in   1999

I Kings 1:1-4
King David was now old, advanced in years;
And though they covered him with bedclothes, he never felt warm.
His courtiers said to him, "Let a young virgin
    be sought for my lord the king,
to wait upon your majesty and be your attendant;
and let her lie in your bosom, and my lord the king will be warm".
So they looked for a beautiful girl throughout the territory of Israel.
They found Abishag the Shunammite and brought her to the king.
The girl was exceedingly beautiful.
She became the king's attendant and waited upon him;
but the king was not intimate with her.

[1]

David and Abishag
39 x 44 in   1999

For what the Bible understands by history is a dialogue in which man, in which the people in the midst of its failure continually rises up and tries to answer. It is the history of God's disappointmnents, but this history of disappointments constitutes a way, a way that leads from disappointment to disappointment and beyond all disappointments; it is the way of the people, the way of man, yes, the way of God through mankind.
Martin Buber, "On the Bible", in *The Man of Today and the Jewish Bible*, Schocken Books, N.Y., 1982

At first I questioned using a dress shop for God's command to Samuel, but moving over to a shoe store strengthened my resolve. Of course the Mahane Yehuda market is a marvelous place with no equal in Jerusalem. I must state that I am the family shopper and can attest to the fact that the market shows distinct improvements in both service and goods. Recently it took on a degree of monumentality with new roofing, although the tin conglomeration before had certain qualities.

"And the Lord said unto Samuel: 'How long wilt thou mourn for Saul..?'"
etching, 25 x 28 cm   1995

page 12

I Samuel 16: 6-13
When they arrived and he saw Eliab, he thought:
"Surely the LORD's anointed stands before Him."
But the LORD said to Samuel, "Pay no attention to his appearance or his stature,
for I have rejected him. For not as man sees does the Lord see;
man sees only what is visible, but the LORD sees into the heart."
Then Jesse called Abinadab and had him pass before Samuel,
but he said, "The LORD has not chosen this one either."
Next Jesse presented Shammah; and again he said,
"The LORD has not chosen this one either."
Thus Jesse presented seven of his sons before Samuel,
and Samuel said to Jesse, "The LORD has not chosen any of these."
Then Samuel asked Jesse, "Are these all the boys you have?"
He replied, "There is still the youngest; he is tending the flock."
And Samuel said to Jesse, "Send someone to bring him,
for we will not sit down to eat until he gets here."
So they sent and brought him. He was ruddy-cheeked, bright-eyed, and handsome.
And the LORD said, "Rise and anoint him, for this is the one."
Samuel took the horn of oil and anointed him in the presence of his brothers;
and the spirit of the LORD gripped David from that day on.
[1]

"Samuel took the horn of oil and anointed him" / green grocer, Mahane Yehuda market
134 x 142 cm   1995

I Samuel 16: 14-20
Now the spirit of the LORD had departed from Saul,
and an evil spirit from the LORD began to terrify him.
Saul's courtiers said to him,
"An evil spirit of God is terrifying you.
Let our lord give the order and the courtiers in attendance on you
will look for someone who is skilled at playing the lyre;
whenever the evil spirit of God comes over you,
he will play it and you will feel better."
So Saul said to his courtiers,
"Find me someone who can play well and bring him to me."
One of the attendants spoke up,
"I have observed a son of Jesse the Bethlehemite
who is skilled in music;
he is a stalwart fellow and a warrior, sensible in speech,
and handsome in appearance, and the LORD is with him."
Whereupon Saul sent messengers to Jesse to say,
"Send me your son David, who is with the flock."
Jesse took an ass laden with bread, a skin of wine, and a kid,
and sent them to Saul by his son David.

[1]

David with gifts for Saul / Jaffa Road near the market
130 x 160 cm   1995

I Samuel 17: 41-49

The Philistine, meanwhile, was coming closer to David, preceded by his shield-bearer.

When the Philistine caught sight of David, he scorned him,

for he was but a boy, ruddy and handsome.

And the Philistine called out to David, "Am I a dog that you come against me with sticks?"

The Philistine cursed David by his gods; and the Philistine said to David,

"Come here, and I will give your flesh to the birds of the sky and the beasts of the field."

David replied to the Philistine, "You come against me with sword and spear and javelin;

but I come against you in the name of the LORD of Hosts,

the God of the ranks of Israel, whom you have defied.

This very day the LORD will deliver you into my hands.

I will kill you and cut off your head;

and I will give the carcasses of the Philistine camp to the birds of the sky

and the beasts of the earth.

All the earth shall know that there is a God in Israel.

And this whole assembly shall know that the LORD can give victory without sword or spear.

For the battle is the LORD's and He will deliver you into our hands."

When the Philistine began to advance toward him again,

David quickly ran up to the battle line to face the Philistine.

David put his hand into the bag; he took out a stone and slung it.

It struck the Philistine in the forehead;

the stone sank into his forehead, and he fell face down on the ground.

[1]

Emek HaElah: The Elah Valley

1010 BCE: David and Goliath

586 BCE: Nebuchadnezzar passes through here

on his way to destroy the Temple in Jerusalem.

200-300 CE: The Romans paved the road to Jerusalem..

634 CE: The Arab Moslems defeat the Roman Byzantine Army.

1773 CE: The Arab shiek Tahar El Omar, conquered

the hills of Hebron from here.

1948 CE: The Egyptian Army passed through

on the way to Jerusalem where it was defeated by the Israeli unit.

Six months later it was established as the border with Jordan

Today: Satellite receptors and light industry dominate the valley.

David and Goliath / Elah Valley today
130 x 162 cm   1995

David and Goliath / Judea
73x92 cm   1979, 1995

David and Goliath / Elah Valley today.
100 x 150   1995

I Samuel 18: 1-4
And it came to pass,
when he had made an end of speaking unto Saul,
that the soul of Jonathan was knit with the soul of David,
and Jonathan loved him as his own soul.
And Saul took him that day,
and would let him go no more to his father's house.
Then Jonathan made a covenant with David,
because he loved him as his own soul.
And Jonathan stripped himself of the robe that was upon him,
and gave it to David,
and his apparel, even to his sword,
and to his bow, and to his girdle.
[2]

Jonathan gives his sword to David
130 x145 cm   1997

1 SAMUEL 18.5-10   DAVID WENT OUT WITH THE TROOPS, AND HE WAS SUCCESSFUL IN EVERY MISSION ON WHICH SAUL SENT HIM, AND SAUL PUT HIM IN COMMAND OF ALL THE SOLDIERS; THIS PLEASED ALL THE TROOPS AND SAUL'S COURTIERS AS WELL. WHEN THE TROOPS CAME HOME AND DAVID RETURNED FROM KILLING THE PHILISTINE, THE WOMEN OF ALL THE TOWNS OF ISRAEL CAME OUT SINGING AND DANCING TO GREET KING SAUL WITH TIMBRELS, SHOUTING, AND SISTRUMS. THE WOMEN SANG AS THEY DANCED, AND THEY CHANTED:
SAUL HAS SLAIN HIS THOUSANDS;
DAVID, HIS TENS OF THOUSANDS!

SAUL WAS MUCH DISTRESSED AND GREATLY VEXED ABOUT THE MATTER. FOR HE SAID, "TO DAVID THEY HAVE GIVEN TENS OF THOUSANDS, AND TO ME THEY HAVE GIVEN THOUSANDS. ALL THAT HE LACKS IS THE KINGSHIP!" FROM THAT DAY ON SAUL KEPT A JEALOUS EYE ON DAVID. THE NEXT DAY AN EVIL SPIRIT OF GOD, GRIPPED SAUL AND HE BEGAN TO RAVE IN THE HOUSE, WHILE DAVID WAS PLAYING THE LYRE, AS HE DID DAILY.   [1]

I am no longer the right model for a youthful David, but an aging Saul is another matter.

David plays for Saul
81 x 100 cm   1995

David plays for Saul
100 x 116 cm   1997

David plays for Saul
116 x 142   1997

I Samuel 19: 1-7

Saul urged his son Jonathan and all his courtiers to kill David.

But Saul's son Jonathan was very fond of David,

and Jonathan told David, "My father Saul is bent on killing you.

Be on your guard tomorrow morning; get to a secret place and remain in hiding.

I will go out and stand next to my father in the field where you will be,

and I will speak to my father about you. If I learn anything, I will tell you."

So Jonathan spoke well of David, to his father Saul. He said to him,

"Let not Your Majesty wrong his servant David, for he has not wronged you;

indeed, all his actions have been very much to your advantage.

He took his life in his hands and killed the Philistine,

and the LORD wrought a great victory for all Israel. You saw it and rejoiced.

Why then should you incur the guilt of shedding the blood of an innocent man,

killing David without cause?"

Saul heeded Jonathan's plea, and Saul swore,

"As the LORD lives, he shall not be put to death!"

Jonathan called David, and Jonathan told him all this.

Then Jonathan brought David to Saul, and he served him as before.

[1]

Jonathan appeals to his father on David's behalf while David hides
160 x 150 cm   1992, 1995

Sept 46
no figures
but the rocks are suspicious
— like a warrior concealed
his parts in with the
pine cones.

I Samuel 19: 8-10
Fighting broke out again. David went out and fought the Philistines.
He inflicted a great defeat upon them and they fled before him.
Then an evil spirit of the LORD came upon Saul
while he was sitting in his house with his spear in his hand, and David was playing [the lyre].
Saul tried to pin David to the wall with the spear, but he eluded Saul,
so that he drove the spear into the wall.
David fled and got away.   [1]

David escapes from King Saul / outside the artist's studio
135 x 153 cm   1981, 1985

David escapes from King Saul / outside the artist's studio
142 x 134 cm   1981, 1996

I Samuel 19: 11-12
That night Saul sent messengers to David's home
to keep watch on him and to kill him in the morning.
But David's wife Michal told him,
"Unless you run for your life tonight, you will be killed tomorrow."
Michal let David down from the window, and he escaped and fled.

[1]

I Samuel 23: 19b-23
Some Ziphites went up to Saul in Gibeah and said,
"David is hiding among us in the strongholds of Horesh,
at the hill of Hachilah south of Jeshimon.
So if Your Majesty has the desire to come down, come down,
and it will be our task to deliver him into Your Majesty's hands."
And Saul replied, "May you be blessed of the LORD for the compassion you have shown me!
Go now and prepare further.
Look around and learn what places he sets foot on and who has seen him there,
for I have been told he is a very cunning fellow.
Look around and learn in which of all his hiding places he has been hiding,
and return to me when you are certain.
I will then go with you, and if he is in the region,
I will search him out among all the clans of Judah."

[1]

David hides from King Saul / Motti's kitchenware, Mahane Yehuda market
143 x 130 cm   1995

I Samuel 23: 24-28
They left at once for Ziph, ahead of Saul;
David and his men were then in the wilderness of Maon,
in the Arabah, to the south of Jeshimon.
When Saul and his men came to search, David was told about it,
and he went down to the rocky region and stayed in the wilderness of Maon.
On hearing this, Saul pursued David in the wilderness of Maon.
Saul was making his way along one side of a hill,
and David and his men were on the other side of the hill.
David was trying hard to elude Saul,
and Saul and his men were trying to encircle David and his men and capture them,
when a messenger came and told Saul,
"Come quickly, for the Philistines have invaded the land."
Saul gave up his pursuit of David and went to meet the Philistines.
That is why that place came to be called the Rock of Separation.

[1]

48

King Saul hunts David
116 x 127 cm   1997

I Samuel 24: 1-16

David went from there and stayed in the wilderness of En-gedi.

When Saul returned from pursuing the Philistines,

he was told that David was in the wilderness of En-gedi.

So Saul took three thousand picked men from all Israel and went in search of David

and his men in the direction of the rocks of the wild goats;

and he came to the sheepfolds along the way.

There was a cave there, and Saul went in to relieve himself.

Now David and his men were sitting in the back of the cave.

David's men said to him, "This is the day of which the LORD said to you,

'I will deliver your enemy into your hands; you can do with him as you please.'"

David went and stealthily cut off the corner of Saul's cloak.

But afterward David reproached himself for cutting off the corner of Saul's cloak.

He said to his men, "The LORD forbid that I should do such a thing to my lord --

the LORD's anointed -- that I should raise my hand against him;

for he is the LORD's anointed."

David rebuked his men and did not permit them to attack Saul.

Saul left the cave and started on his way. Then David also went out of the cave

and called after Saul, "My lord king!"

Saul looked around and David bowed low in homage, with this face to the ground.

And David said to Saul, "Why do you listen to the people who say,

'David is out to do you harm?' You can see for yourself now that the LORD

delivered you into my hands in the cave today.

And though I was urged to kill you, I showed you pity, for I said,

'I will not raise a hand against my lord, since he is the LORD's anointed.'

Please, sir, take a close look at the corner of your cloak in my hand;

for when I cut off the corner of your cloak, I did not kill you.

You must see plainly that I have done nothing evil or rebellious,

and I have never wronged you.

Yet you are bent on taking my life. May the LORD judge between you and me!

And may He take vengeance upon you for me, but my hand will never touch you.

As the ancient proverb has it: 'Wicked deeds come from wicked men!'

My hand will never touch you.

Against whom has the king of Israel come out?

Whom are you pursuing? A dead dog? A single flea?

May the LORD be arbiter and may He judge between you and me!

May He take note and uphold my cause, and vindicate me against you."

[1]

One day as David was seated on the roof he saw a hornet eating a spider. He began to muse "What purpose did God have in creating these insects? The hornet spoils the honey and brings no benefit to anything, while the spider can spin all year long and not weave a single garment!" God answered, "David, don't be so quick in your judgement. The day will come when you will have need of these insects!"

Later when David hid in the cave to escape King Saul, God sent a spider which wove a web over the entrance of the cave. When Saul noticed the spider's web over the mouth of the cave, he said "No one could be inside, since whoever entered would have broken the web." And Saul left the site without investigating any further. When David left the cave and saw the spider and its web, he exclaimed to the spider, "Blessed is He who created you and blessed are you!"

Sefer Ha-aggadah, The Book of Jewish Folklore and Legend by H.N Bialik and Y.H. Ravnitzky, Dvir 1988, Tel Aviv

David cuts off the corner of Saul's cloak / Judean terraces
132 x 122 cm   1995

I Samuel 24: 17-23

When David finished saying these things to Saul, Saul said,
"Is that your voice, my son David?"
And Saul broke down and wept.
He said to David, "You are right, not I; for you have treated me generously,
but I have treated you badly.
Yes, you have just revealed how generously you treated me,
for the LORD delivered me into your hands and you did not kill me.
If a man meets his enemy, does he let him go his way unharmed?
Surely, the LORD will reward you generously
for what you have done for me this day.
I know now that you will become king,
and the kingship over Israel will remain in your hands.
So swear to me by the LORD that you will not destroy my descendants
or wipe out my name from my father's house."
David swore to Saul,
Saul went home, and David and his men went up to the strongholds.

[1]

"Is that your voice, my son David?"
162 x 135 cm   1996

I Samuel 31: 1-13
The Philistines attacked Israel,
and the men of Israel fled before the Philistines
and many fell on Mount Gilboa.
The Philistines pursued Saul and his sons,
and the Philistines struck down Jonathan, Abinadab, and Malchi-shua, sons of Saul.
The battle raged around Saul,
and some of the archers hit him,
and he was severely wounded by the archers.
Saul said to his arms-bearer,
"Draw your sword and run me through,
so that the uncircumcised may not run me through and make sport of me."
But his arms-bearer, in his great awe, refused;
whereupon Saul grasped the sword and fell upon it.
When his arms bearer saw that Saul was dead,
he too fell on his sword and died with him.
Thus Saul and his three sons and his arms-bearer, as well as all his men,
died together on that day.
And when the men of Israel on the other side of the valley
and on the other side of the Jordan
saw that the men of Israel had fled
and that Saul and his sons were dead,
they abandoned the towns and fled;
the Philistines then came and occupied them.

The next day the Philistines came to strip the slain,
and they found Saul and his three sons lying on Mount Gilboa.
They cut off his head and stripped him of his armor,
and they sent them throughout the land of the Philistines,
to spread the news in the temples of their idols and among the people.
They placed his armor in the temple of Ashtaroth,
and they impaled his body on the wall of Beth-shan.
When the inhabitants of Jabesh-gilead heard about it
-- what the Philistines had done to Saul --
all their stalwart men set out and marched all night;
they removed the bodies of Saul and his sons from the well of Beth-shan
and came to Jabesh and burned them there.
Then they took the bones and buried them under the tamarisk tree in Jabesh,
and they fasted for seven days.

[1]

Saul falls upon his sword / Mount Gilboa
92 x 116 cm   1995

Saul is dead.
David is now King.
He will shepherd, provide
and feed his people
and then conquer
Jerusalem.

Safba Road

and with a combination of
political skill and
religious fervor, bring
into his new capital the
Ark of the Covenant

II Samuel 5: 1-5
Then came all the tribes of Israel, to David unto Hebron,
and spake, saying, Behold, we are thy bone and thy flesh.
Also in time past, when Saul was king over us,
thou wast he that leddest out and broughtest in Israel:
and the Lord said to thee,
Thou shalt feed my people Israel,
and thou shalt be a captain over Israel.

So all the elders of Israel came to the king to Hebron;
and king David made a league with them in Hebron before the Lord:
and they anointed David king over Israel.

David was thirty years old when he began to reign,
and he reigned forty years.
In Hebron he reigned over Judah seven years and six months:
and in Jerusalem he reigned thirty and three years
over all Israel and Judah.
[4]

"Thou shalt feed my people Israel" / Mahane Yehuda market
150 x 135 cm   1995

Amir Hirschenson's father sat in my studio in front of this painting talking to his son.
He said, "Schwebel's drawing is different from the photograph
because I see the old tear-duct blockage of your childhood".
This was a few months after Amir was killed by a terrorist bomb at Bet Lid on January 22,1995.

"Thou shalt feed my people Israel" / Mahane Yehuda market
116 x 130 cm   1995

61

II Samuel 6: 12-19
It was reported to King David: "The LORD has blessed Obed-edom's house
and all that belongs to him
because of the Ark of God."
Thereupon David went and brought up the Ark of God
from the house of Obed-edom to the City of David, amid rejoicing.
When the bearers of the Ark of the LORD had moved forward six paces,
he sacrificed an ox and a fatling.
David whirled with all his might before the LORD;
David was girt with a linen ephod.
Thus David and all the House of Israel brought up the Ark of the LORD
with shouts and with blasts of the horn.
As the Ark of the LORD entered the City of David,
Michal daughter of Saul looked out of the window and saw King David leaping
and whirling before the LORD; and she despised him for it.

They brought in the Ark of the LORD
and set it up in its place inside the tent which David had pitched for it,
and David sacrificed burnt offerings and offerings of well-being before the LORD.
When David finished sacrificing the burnt offerings and the offerings of well-being,
he blessed the people in the name of the LORD of Hosts.
And he distributed among all the people
-- the entire multitude of Israel, man and woman alike --
to each a loaf of bread, a cake made in a pan, and a raisin cake.
Then all the people left for their homes.

[1]

"David whirls with all his might before the Lord" / Jerusalem's Zion Square, Jaffa Road
135 x 160 cm   1983, 1996

David whirls with the
ark on Zion Square,
up and down the
crossings, from the
Old City westward
to Mahane Yehuda
and further,
much further

From Yehuda Amichai's introduction to the second edition of *The Arena of Jerusalem:*

We sing "David, King of Israel, is alive and exists." To believers, this verse heralds the everlastingness of the House of David and the coming of the Messiah, Son of David. Schwebel gives this verse a real and piercing significance, as only a great artist can. He has taken the stories of David from thousands of years ago, and transferred them like a live production to the streets of present-day Jerusalem. It is obvious that he is not painting the classical Jerusalem, or the tourist's Jerusalem, or the famous Jerusalem of the Old City, Mea Shearim and the Mount of Olives, but rather Jaffa Road, King George and Ben Yehuda with their petit bourgeois stores and their rather ugly houses. Against this background David dances [whirls], David laments, David commits adultery and loves, cries, laughs, hates and flatters. And just as the background is self-evident, so is the fact that King David is Schwebel with his friends and family, his loves and hates serving as Batsheva, Uriyya the Hittite, Michal, Shimei, Amnon and Tamar, and Absalom. Someone looking at these painting understands the Bible and Jerusalem more deeply. And behold, a person looking at these paintings and internalizing them becomes an artist himself.

"David whirls with all his might before the Lord" / Jaffa Road, Zion Square
160 x 150 cm   1982

"David whirls with all his might before the Lord" / Mahane Yehuda market
134 x 143 cm   1995

778

28 July, Weds.
TISH A BAAV

Getting the mush paint
to behave and offer itself
up to the Heroic Man.
who is becoming a
Dancing David or else
a mournful one.
Heavy paint envelopes
him and he eats light
meals off it.

It invents myths,
picks up the
dragons and lions
and angry gods
on its path.

from my journals

70

"David whirls with all his might before the Lord" / The Tourjeman House on Route #1
150 x 130 cm   1996

This building served as an outpost and checkpoint for the Israel Defence Forces in the
divided city of Jerusalem between 1948 and 1967. Next to it was the Mandlebaum Gate,
the only passageway between Israel and Jordan during these 20 years. The building is now a museum.

Some great force gets him to whirl (dance)
with the Ark of the Covenant into his newly
conquered capital. And he agrees, takes full
responsibility for it. Surely he enjoys his
mission and his power to make use of it.

John Berryman's poem, "King David Dances":
Aware to the dry throat of the wide hell in the world,
O trampling empires, and mine one of them,
and mine one gross desire against His sight,
slaughter devising there,
some good behind, ambiguous ahead,
revolted sons, a pierced son, bound to bear,
mid hypocrites amongst idolaters,
mockt in abysm by one shallow wife,
with the ponder both of priesthood and of State
heavy upon me, yea,
all the black same I dance my blue head off!

David whirls / Ben Yehuda Street
etching, actual size   1981

David whirls / Jaffa Road
etching, 100 x 100 cm   1994

November '94

David whirls
in front of
Deportation Trains
and the Wire
of Concentration
Camps.

He's got to do that
for us, break up
the horror, if
he's the man
we believe
him to be.

The following pages include selections from my book, *The Inescapable*, a portrayal of Jewish experience from 14th century Spain into the Holocaust, as yet unpublished.

David whirls / barbed wire on a Bronx street
painted etching, 80 x 65 cm   1993

As regards the lords of evil, the curiosity, which is not limited to the Nazi chiefs, still lingers. Hundreds of books have come out on the psychology of Hitler, Stalin, Himmler, Goebbels, and I have read dozens of them and have been left unsatisfied: but probably it is a matter here of the essential inadequacy of documentary evidence. It almost never has the power to give us the depths of a human being; for this purpose the dramatists or poet are more appropriate than the historian or psychologist.
Primo Levi, *Moments of Reprieve*, Abacus, 1987

David whirls / Deportation Train containing Zion Square
130 x130 cm   1987, 1992

Here then before our very eyes, under our very feet, was one of those notorious transportation
trains, those which never return, and of which, shuddering and always a little incredulous,
we had so often heard speak. Exactly like this, detail for detail; goods, wagons, closed from
the outside, with men, women and children pressed together without pity, like cheap
merchandise for a journey towards nothingness, a journey, down there towards the bottom.
This time it was us who are inside.
Primo Levi, *If This Is A Man*, Abacus, 1987

David and Jesus (after El Greco) / Auschwitz barbed wire
134 x 142   1992

David whirls / Auschwitz arrival platform
151 x 111 cm   1992

It was that shame we knew so well, the shame that drowned us after the selections, and every time we had to watch, or submit to, some outrage the shame the Germans did not know, that the just man experiences at another man's crime; the feeling of guilt that such a crime should exist, that it should have been introduced irrevocably into the world of things that exist, and that his will for good should have proved too weak or null, and should not have availed in defence. Primo Levi, *The Truce*, Abacus, 1987

David whirls / Auschwitz arrival platform
111 x 151 cm   1992

Part of Daniel Marom's essay in *The Inescapable*:
For centuries, poets, artists, mystics and teachers have returned to the image of David in
order to rediscover their own vitality, to "renew their days of old." It is David's eternal youth,
his overflowing daring and spontaneity, his irresistible mixture of sensual primacy and religious
integrity which makes him the lasting prototype for the Messianic King and a figurehead for
renaissance. When all else withers, the memory of David remains the source of life. By
remembering David, one forgets the sinful, the decrepit, and the ruined, and moves on to the
next venture.
But it is not an easy victory. For all his hardships, David did not have to see his city ravished
and burned, nor his temple destroyed and mocked. He did not have to suffer the humiliation
of his would-be-king descendants, to witness their being ridiculed, enslaved, crucified, burned
at the stake and transformed into farcical reminders of the hopelessness of restoring his reign.
...Who, after the Holocaust, can rely on David anymore without asking him to take some of the
blows too, without letting him see what has to be done in order to stay alive? Who can protect
him any longer from what our eyes have seen? Whether for love of David or for fear of losing
him, Schwebel could no longer live with him without taking him through this terrible ordeal.

From Yehuda Halevi's "Ode to Zion":
O Zion, will you not ask how your captives are --
the exiles who seek your welfare,
who are from the remnant of your flocks?
From west and east, north and south, from every side,
accept the greetings of those near and far,
and the blessings of this captive of desire,
who sheds his tears like the dew of Hermon
and longs to have them fall upon your hills,
I am like a jackal when I weep for your affliction;
but when I dream of your exiles' return,
I am a lute for your songs.

Yehuda Halevi (c. 1075-1141).   The Hebrew poet and philosopher, was born and educated in Moslem Spain.   His poems were about theology, love and wine. The invading Christians persecuted the Jews, causing him to reflect deeply on the humiliation of his people. In search of a redeeming act, Halevi decided late in life to emigrate to Israel, which he believed was the only place in which ideal Jewish existence could be attained.   There is scant evidence that he reached his destination: "I have it from an old man that when he reached the gates of Jerusalem, he tore his clothes and walked barefoot on the ground in order to fulfill the verse that says: 'For the time is come for thy servants to take pleasure in her stones, and favor the dust thereof' (Psalm 102); whereupon an Ismaelite was overcome with jealousy for Halevi's passion, went over to him with his horse and trampled him to death."

From Heinrich Heine's poem "Hebrew Melodies":
But a Saracen came riding
Brazen-souled along the roadway;
Rocking back high on his charger,
Down he swung a shining lance
Into the poor singer's bosom
And the deadly shaft was fatal;
Then he rode off at a gallop
Like a shape of winged shadow.

David whirls / Jehuda Halevi and the Ismaelite / Agrippas Street at the market
150 x 200 cm   1991

II Samuel 6: 20-23
David went home to greet his household.
And Michal daughter of Saul came out to meet David and said,
"Didn't the king of Israel do himself honor today
-- exposing himself today in the sight of the slavegirls of his subjects,
as one of the riffraff might expose himself!"
David answered Michal, "It was before the LORD
who chose me instead of your father and all his family
and appointed me ruler over the LORD's people Israel!
I will dance before the LORD and dishonor myself even more,
and be low in my own esteem;
but among the slavegirls that you speak of I will be honored."
So to her dying day Michal daughter of Saul had no children.

[1]

The Bible knows nothing of the intrinsic value of success. On the contrary, when it announces a successful deed, it is duty-bound to announce in complete detail the failure involved in the success. Or let us consider the life of David. So far as we are told of it, it consists essentially of two great stories of flight. Before his accession to the throne there are the manifold accounts of his flight from Saul, and then follows an interruption which is not trifling in terms of length and its value for profane history, but which in the account appears paltry enough, and after this there is the flight from Absalom, painted for us in detail. And even where the Bible recounts David's triumph, as for instance with the entry of the Ark in Jerusalem, this triumph is clearly described as a disgrace in a worldly sense; this is very unlike the language of world history. What Michal, his wife, says to David of his triumph, that he ought to have felt ashamed of himself behaving as he did in front of his people (II Samuel 6:20) -- that is the language of profane history, i.e., of history *par excellence.* To history, such a royal appearance is not permitted, and rightly so, seeing that history is what it is.
Martin Buber, On The Bible", in *The Man of Today and the Jewish Bible,* Schocken Books, 1982.

Michal and David / Jaffa Road
89 x 100 cm   1985

Michal and David / Jaffa Road
65 x 100 cm   1985

II Samuel 7: 1-3
When the king was settled in his palace
and the LORD had granted him safety from all the enemies around him,
the king said to the prophet Nathan:
"Here I am dwelling in a house of cedar, while the Ark of the LORD abides in a tent!"
Nathan said to the king,
"Go and do whatever you have in mind, for the LORD is with you."

[1]

Natan and David: The Question of the Temple / Mahane Yehuda market
164 x 130 cm   1995

II Samuel 7: 4-21
But that same night the word of the LORD came to Nathan:
"Go and say to My servant David:
Thus said the LORD: Are you the one to build a house for Me to dwell in?
From the day that I brought the people of Israel out of Egypt to this day
I have not dwelt in a house,
but have moved about in Tent and Tabernacle.
As I moved wherever the Israelites went,
did I ever reproach any of the tribal leaders
whom I appointed to care for My people Israel:
Why have you not built Me a house of cedar?

"Further, say thus to My servant David:
Thus said the LORD of Hosts:
I took you from the pasture, from following the flock,
to be ruler of My people Israel,
and I have been with you wherever you went,
and have cut down all your enemies before you.
Moreover, I will give you great renown like that of the greatest men on earth.
I will establish a home for My people Israel and will plant them firm,
so that they shall dwell secure and shall tremble no more.
Evil men shall not oppress them any more as in the past,
ever since I appointed chieftains over My people Israel.
I will give you safety from all your enemies.
The LORD declares to you that He, the LORD, will establish a house for you.
When your days are done and you lie with your fathers,
I will raise up your offspring after you, one of your own issue,
and I will establish his kingship.
He shall build a house for My name,
and I will establish his royal throne forever.
I will be a father to him, and he shall be a son to Me.
When he does wrong, I will chastise him with the rod of men
and the affliction of mortals;
but I will never withdraw My favor from him as I withdrew it from Saul,
whom I removed to make room for you.
Your house and your kingship shall ever be secure before you;
your throne shall be established forever."

Nathan spoke to David in accordance with all these words and all this prophecy.
Then King David came and sat before the LORD, and he said,
"What am I, O Lord GOD, and what is my family, that You have brought me thus far?
Yet even this, O Lord GOD, has seemed too little to You;
for You have spoken of Your servant's house also for the future.
May that be the law for the people, O Lord GOD.
What more can David say to You?
You know Your servant, O Lord GOD.
For Your word's sake and of Your own accord You have wrought this great thing,
and made it known to Your servant..."

[1]

"King David came and sat before the Lord" / Mahane Yehuda market entrance
146 x 116 cm   1995

"King David came and sat before the Lord" / Jaffa Road and Strauss Street
130 x 150 cm   1995

Sitting in prayer in God's presence or without is not mentioned elsewhere in the Bible.
This appears to be the special privilege of David.
Both paintings, one of anger, one of pain, were painted soon after the murder of Yitzhak Rabin.

"King David came and sat before the Lord" / Jaffa Road and Strauss Street
134 x 110 cm   1995

II Samuel 11: 1-5
Now it was at the turn of the year, at the time when kings go out:
David sent Yoav and his officers with him and all Israel,
they destroyed the land of the Sons of Ammon and beseiged Rabbah;
but David remained in Jerusalem.
Now it was around even-time:
David arose from where-he-lay and went for a walk upon the roof
      of the king's house,
and he saw a woman washing herself, from the roof,
the woman was extremely fair to look at.
David sent and had inquiry made after the woman,
they said: Is this not Bat-sheva, daughter of Eli'am, wife of Uriyya the Hittite?
David sent messengers, and she was taken,
she came to him and he lay with her --
now she had just made herself holy from her period --
then she returned to her house.
The woman became pregnant,
she sent and had it told to David, she said: I am pregnant!
                              [5]

The meeting of the Judean hills with the plain has always been dramatic. Shaar Hagay -- literally "the Gate of the Valley" -- is one of the better known meeting points. Ruins in the area show that it was a major way-station between the coast and Jerusalem since Roman times. When European travellers were allowed to visit Palestine at the beginning of the 19th century, it was reported that 100 camels a day would pass through Shaar Hagay. The Turks built a fortress there to ensure the safety of the travellers, for a toll, and in 1869 paved the first stone road from there to Jerusalem. The municipality of Jerusalem built a hotel there, the remnants of which stands opposite the Paz gas station on one's right in the ascent to Jerusalem. It was leased to a Jewish family and called "The Judean Hills Hotel". The laying of the Jaffa -- Jerusalem railroad line and the asphalt paving of the road put the hotel out of business but the strategic importance of the route was only enhanced. The first 6 kilometers from Shaar Hagay towards Jerusalem were the site of intense fighting between the Arab Legion and the Israeli Defense Forces duringthe 1948 War of Independence. There is a popular song often on the air about these battles with Shaar Hagay's Arabic name "Bab El Wad", as its title.

"He saw a woman washing herself" / Shaar Hagay

146 x 162 cm   1997

"He saw a woman washing herself" / From a roof over Shlomzion Hamalka Street
etching, Actual size   1981

"He saw a woman washing herself" / over Ein Karem, Jerusalem
130 x 150 cm   1996

"David sent messengers, and she was taken" / over Shlomzion Hamalka Street
60 x 92 cm   1979, 1996

"She had just made herself holy from her period" / across the valley from Mt. Zion
135 x 150 cm   1995

II Samuel 11: 6-11
David sent to Yoav: Send me Uriyyah the Hittite.
Yoav sent Uriyya to David.
When Uriyya came to him, David asked after the well-being of Yoav,
    the well-being of the people, and the well-being of the battle,
then David said to Uriyya:
Go down to your house and wash your feet.
Uriyyah went out of the king's house,
after him went a portion from the king.
but Uriyyah lay down at the entrance to the king's house,
with all his lord's officers, he did not go down to his house.
They told David saying: Uriyya has not gone down to his house.
David said to Uriyya: Is it not from a long journey that you have come?
Why have you not gone down to your house?
Uriyyah said to David: The Ark and Israel and Judah stay in huts,
my lord Yoav and my lord's officers are encamped on the surface of the field,
and I, I should come into my house, to eat, and drink, and lie with my wife?!
As you live, and as your soul lives: Were I to do this thing...!

[5]

II Samuel 11: 12-17
David said to Uriyya: Remain here today also, toworrow I will send you back.
So Uriyya remained in Jerusalem on that day.
On the morrow David had him called,
to eat and drink in his presence, and he made him intoxicated.
But he went out in the evening to lie down in his lying place with his lord's servants;
to his house he did not go down.

So it was in the morning:
David wrote a letter to Yoav and sent it by hand to Uriyya,
he wrote in the letter, saying:
Bring Uriyya right to front of the battle, the strongest point,
and turn back behind him, so that he is struck down and dies.

So it was:
When Yoav had scouted out the city,
he put Uriyya at the place where he knew that there were men of caliber.
When the men of the city went out to fight with Yoav,
there fell some of the people, of David's officers,
and there also died Uriyya the Hittite.

II Samuel 11: 26,27
When Uriyya's wife heard that her man was dead,
she mourned for her husband.
But when the mourning past, David sent and had her brought to his house;
she became his wife, and bore him a son.
But the thing that David had done was evil in the eyes of YHWH.
[5]

David gets Uriyya drunk / Ben Yehuda Street
150 x 160 cm   1983

David gets Uriyya drunk / Jaffa Road
150 x 160   1983

This reason has been given for David's strong attempt to get Uriyyah to bed Batsheva:
her punishment for adultery would have been death.

David gets Uriyya drunk / Sergio's Restaurant, Agrippas Street
153 x 134 cm   1995

II Samuel 12: 1-14
Now YHWH sent Natan to David,
he came to him and said to him:
There were two men in a city,
one rich and one poor.
The rich-one had sheep and oxen, very many,
but the poor-one had nothing at all save one little lamb
which he had bought and kept alive;
it grew up with him, together with his children:
from his morsel it ate,
from his cup it drank,
in his bosom it lay;
it was to him like a daughter.
Now there came a journey-goer to the rich man,
but he thought it a pity to take from his sheep or from his oxen,
    to make something ready for the wayfarer that had come to him,
so he took the poor man's lamb and made it ready for the man who had come to him,
David's anger burned greatly against the man,
he said to Natan: As YHWH lives,
indeed, worthy of death is the man who does thus!
For the lamb he shall pay sevenfold -
because he did such a thing, and since he had no pity!
Natan said to David:
You are the man!
Thus say YHWH, the God of Israel:
I myself anointed you king over Israel,
I myself rescued you from the hand of Sha'ul,
I gave you the house of Israel and Judah;
and as if that were too little, I added yet this and that to you:
Why have you mocked the word of YHWH, to do what is evil in my eyes?
Uriyya the Hittite you have struck down by the sword;
his wife you have taken for yourself as a wife,
and him you have killed by the sword of the Sons of Ammon.
And now - never shall the sword depart from your house,
because you mocked me and took the wife of Uriyya the Hittite to be a wife for you.
Thus says YHWH:

Here, I will raise up against	your (person)
evil from	your house
I will take away	your wives
from before	your eyes
I will give them to	your fellow
and he shall lie with	your wives,

under the eyes of this sun.
For you, you did it in secret,
but I, I will do this thing before all Israel, and before the sun.
David said to Natan: I have sinned against YHWH!
Natan said to David: YHWH has also let your sin pass,
you will not die; nevertheless,
since you have sneered, yes, sneered at "YHWH's enemies" by doing this thing,
also the son who is born to you: he must die, yes, die.

[5]

"I have sinned against YHWH!" / Mahane Yehuda market
89 x 100 cm   199

II Samuel 12: 15-19
Now YHWH smote the newborn child that Uriyya's wife had borne to David,
　　so that he took sick.
David besought God on behalf of the boy,
and David fasted a fast:
whenever he came home, he spent the night lying upon the earth.
The elders of his house arose about him to raise him up from the earth,
but he was unwilling and would not refresh himself in food with them.
Now it was on the seventh day: the child died.

David's servants were afraid to tell him that the child was dead, for they said:
Here, while the child was still alive, we spoke to him and he did not listen to our voice.
So how can we say to him: the child is dead? He might do evil!
When David saw that his servants were whispering to one another,
David knew that the child was dead.
David said to his servants:
Is the child dead?
They said: It is dead.
[5]

II Samuel 12: 20-23
Then David arose from the earth,
he washed, anointed himself, changed his clothes,
and came into the house of YHWH and prostrated himself.
He came back to his house, asked that they put food before him, and ate.
His servants said to him: What kind of thing is this that you do?
For the sake of the living child, you fasted and wept,
and now that the child is dead, you arise, you eat food!
He said: As long as the child still lives, I fasted, I wept,
for I said to myself: Who knows, perhaps YHWH will be gracious to me, and the child will live!
But now that he is dead, why should I fast? Can I make him return again?
I may go to him, but he will not return to me.   [5]

"David arose from the earth" / Broadway near Canal Street, N.Y.
painted etching, 50 x 50 cm   1995

"David arose from the earth" / Zion Square
135 x 110 cm   1983

"David arose from the earth" / Jaffa Road and King George Street
etching, 23 x 27 cm   1986

"David arose from the earth" / Zion Square and the lone trolley of the Warsaw Ghetto
130 x 160 cm   1994

Chaim Rumkovski's order to the Jews of the Lodz Ghetto (from *The Inescapable*):

Lately it has been noted repeatedly that the previously ordered obligation to salute all German officials is not being carried out. I am warning you again that all German officials in uniform and in plain clothes are to be greeted by residents of the Ghetto. The obligation to salute also applies to cars that are passing through.

   Ch. Rumkovski

   The Eldest of the Jews in Litzmannstadt (Lodz)

   [otherwise known as "The King of the Jews"]

II Samuel 12: 24,25
David comforted Bat-sheva his wife,
he came to her and lay with her.
She bore a son and called his name Shelomo (Solomon).
YHWH loved him and had him sent into the hand of Natan the prophet;
he called his name Yedidya / Beloved of YHWH, for the sake of YHWH.   [5]

David and Batsheva console one another
etching, actual size   1995

"Jedidah" means the Lord's beloved, a name given as a pledge to David that
this child of Batsheva would not suffer the consequences of his sin as did the first.

David consoles Batsheva / Zion Square
etching, 100 x100 cm   1994

113

II Samuel 13: 1-14
In the course of time,
Amnon son of David fell in love with Tamar,
the beautiful sister of Absalom son of David.
Amnon became frustrated to the point of illness on account of his sister Tamar,
for she was a virgin,
and it seemed impossible to do anything to her.

Now Amnon had a friend named Jonadab son of Shimeah, David's brother.
Jonadab was a very shrewd man.
He asked Amnon,
"Why do you, the king's son, look so haggard morning after morning?
Won't you tell me?"
Amon said to him,
I'm in love with Tamar, my brother Absalom's sister.
"Go to bed and pretend to be ill," Jonadab said.
"When your father comes to see you, say to him,
'I would like my sister Tamar to come and give me something to eat.
Let her prepare the food in my sight so that I may watch her
and then eat it from her hand.'"
So Amnon lay down and pretended to be ill.
When the king came to see him, Amnon said to him,
"I would like my sister Tamar to come and give me something to eat.
Let her prepare the food in my sight so that I may watch her
and then eat it from her hand."
David sent word to Tamar at the palace:
"Go to the house of your brother Amnon and prepare some food for him."
So Tamar went to the house of her brother Amnon, who was lying down.
She took some dough, kneaded it, made the bread in his sight and baked it.
Then she took the pan and served him the bread, but he refused to eat.
"Send everyone out of here," Amnon said.
So everyone left him.
Then Amnon said to Tamar,
"Bring the food here into my bedroom so that I might eat from your hand".
And Tamar took the bread she had prepared
and brought it to her brother Amnon in his bedroom.
But when she took it to him to eat, he grabbed her and said,
"Come to bed with me, my sister".
"Don't, my brother!" she said to him.
"Don't force me. Such a thing should not be done in Israel!
Don't do this wicked thing.
What about me? Where could I get rid of my disgrace?
And what about you? You would be like one of the wicked fools in Israel.
Please speak to the king; he will not keep me from being married to you."
But he refused to listen to her,
and since he was stronger than she, he raped her.

[3]

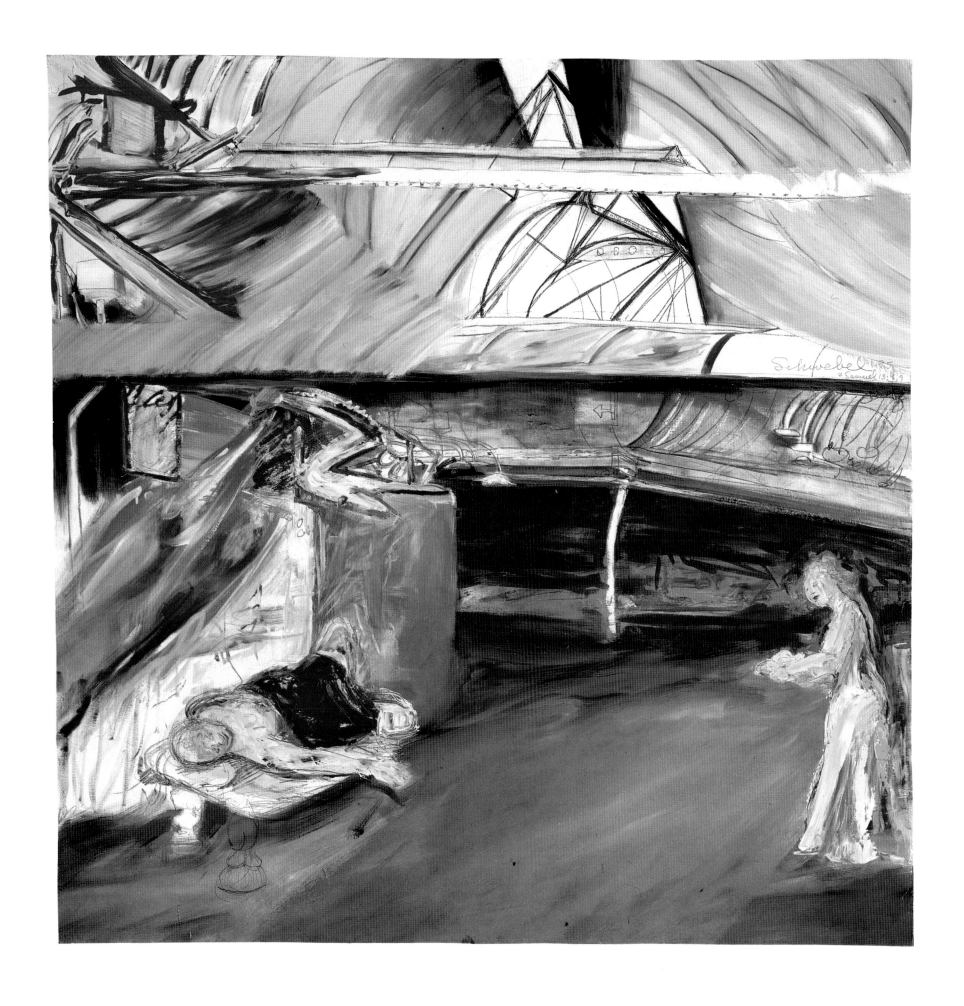

The rape of Tamar: "Bring the food inside and feed me" / Mahane Yehuda market
162 x 162 cm   1995

II Samuel 13: 15-22
Then Amnon hated her with intense hatred.
In fact, he hated her more than he had loved her.
Amnon said to her, "Get up and get out!
"No! she said to him.
"Sending me away would be a greater wrong
than what you have already done to me."
But he refused to listen to her.
He called his personal servant and said,
"Get this woman out of here
and bolt the door after her."
So his servant put her out
and bolted the door after her.
She was wearing a richly ornamented robe,
for this was the kind of garment
the virgin daughters of the king wore.
Tamar put ashes on her head
and tore the ornamented robe she was wearing.
She put her hand on her head and she went away,
weeping aloud as she went.
Her brother Absalom said to her,
"Has that Amnon, your brother, been with you?
Be quiet now, my sister; he is your brother.
Don't take this thing to heart."
And Tamar lived in her brother Absalom's house,
a desolate woman.
When King David heard all this, he was furious.
Absalom never said a word to Amnon,
either good or bad; he hated Amnon
because he had disgraced his sister Tamar.

[3]

The rape of Tamar: "Tamar put ashes on her head and tore the ornamented robe" / Zion Square
160 x 135 cm   1983

The rape of Tamar: "Tamar put ashes on her head and tore the ornamented robe" / Zion Square
160 x 135 cm   1983

THE LAST DAYS OF THE
ZION CINEMA 1984

II Samuel 14: 25-27
No one in all Israel was so admired for his beauty as Absalom;
from the sole of his foot to the crown of his head he was without blemish.
When he cut his hair --
he had to have it cut every year, for it grew too heavy for him
-- the hair of his head weighed two hundred shekels by the royal weight.

[1]

The Zion Cinema was torn down around 1983. Sheltered under its marquee was a famous meeting-place for Jerusalemites. The cinema was also the scene for Independence celebrations and terrorist bombs.

II Samuel 15: 1-6

Sometime afterward, Absalom provided himself with a chariot,
horses, and fifty outrunners.
Absalom used to rise early and stand by the road to the city gates;
and whenever a man had a case that was to come before the king for judgment,
Absalom would call out to him, "What town are you from?"
And when he answered, "Your servant is from such and such a tribe in Israel,"
Absalom would say to him, "It is clear that your claim is right and just,
but there is no one assigned to you by the king to hear it."
And Absalom went on, "If only I were appointed judge in the land
and everyone with a legal dispute came before me, I would see that he got his rights."
And if a man approached to bow to him,
Absalom would extend his hand and take hold of him and kiss him.
Absalom did this to every Israelite who came to the king for judgment.
Thus Absalom won away the hearts of the men of Israel.

[1]

"Absalom would extend his hand and... kiss him"
89 x 116 cm   1996

120

"Absalom used to rise early and stand by the road" / Mea Shearim
100 x 116 cm   1995

2 SAMUEL 15. 30

DAVID MEANWHILE WENT UP THE SLOPE OF THE MOUNT OF OLIVES, WEEPING AS HE WENT; HIS HEAD WAS COVERED AND HE WALKED BAREFOOT. AND ALL THE PEOPLE WHO WERE WITH HIM COVERED THEIR HEADS AND WEPT AS THEY WENT UP...

[1]

David escapes from Absalom up the Mount of Olives
150 x 130 cm   1995

II Samuel 16: 5-8
As King David was approaching Bahurim, a member of Saul's clan
-- a man named Shimei son of Gera --
came out from there, hurling insults as he came.
He threw stones at David and all King David's courtiers,
while all the troops and all the warriors were at his right and his left.
And these are the insults that Shimei hurled:
"Get out, get out, you criminal, you villain!
The LORD is paying you back for all your crimes
against the family of Saul, whose throne you seized.
The LORD is handing over the throne to your son Absalom,
you are in trouble because you are a criminal!"

[1]

Brony Street with a
Judean hill descending

march 4 '83   135 X 150

I return to Shimei throwing stones at David
and his entourage. Accounts to settle amongst
Israelis!
Big Ed Walsh, 1909 White Sox pitcher, stands in
for Shimei. He has just thrown one in front
of Egged Tours. He throws westward, aiming
past the 4 men guarding David, who is not
seen in the painting.
        The question is should I leave in the "Sox"
and glove since I am so careful about the
identity of the mercedes taxi?

from my journals

"Shimei threw stones at David" / Jaffa Road
135 x 150 cm   1983

"Shimei threw stones at David" / Zion Square
painted etching, 100 x 100 cm   1995

"Shimei threw stones at David" / Zion Square
110 x 135 cm   1983

II Samuel 16: 20-23

Absalom then said to Ahithophel, "What do you advise us to do?"

And Ahithophel said to Absalom, "Have intercourse with your father's concubines,

whom he left to mind the palace;

and when all Israel hears that you have dared the wrath of your father,

all who support you will be encouraged."

So they pitched a tent for Absalom on the roof,

and Absalom lay with his father's concubines

with the full knowledge of all Israel.

[1]

"Absalom lay with his father's concubines" / from a roof over Shlomzion Hamalka Street

etching, actual size   1981

130

"Absalom lay with his father's concubines" / from a roof over Shlomzion Hamalka Street
61 x 89 cm   1979, 1996

II Samuel 18: 5-10
...The king gave orders to Joab, Abishai, and Ittai:
"Deal gently with my boy Absalom, for my sake."
All the troops heard the king give the order about Absalom to all the officers
The troops marched out into the open to confront the Israelites,
and the battle was fought in the forest of Ephraim.
The Israelite troops were routed by David's followers,
and a great slaughter took place there that day -- twenty thousand men.
The battle spread out over that whole region,
and the forest devoured more troops that day than the sword.
Absalom encountered some of David's followers.
Absalom was riding on a mule,
and as the mule passed under the tangled branches of a great terebinth,
his hair got caught in the terebinth;
he was held between heaven and earth
as the mule under him kept going.

One of the men saw it and told Joab,
"I have just seen Absalom hanging from a terebinth."
Joab said to the man who told him,
"You saw it! Why didn't you kill him then and there?
I would have owed you ten shekels of silver and a belt."
But the man answered Joab, "Even if I had a thousand shekels of silver in my hands,
I would not raise a hand against the king's son.
For the king charged you and Abishai and Ittai in our hearing,
'Watch over my boy Absalom, for my sake.' If I betrayed myself --
and nothing is hidden from the king -- you would have stood aloof."
Joab replied, "Then I will not wait for you."
He took three darts in his hand and drove them into Absalom's chest.
Absalom was still alive in the thick growth of the terebinth,
when ten of Yoav's young arms-bearers closed in
and struck at Absalom until he died.

[1]

II Samuel 18: 24-32
David was sitting between the two gates.
The watchman on the roof of the gate
walked over to the city wall.
He looked up and saw a man running alone.
The watchman called down and told the king;
and the king said, "If he is alone, he has news to report."
As he was coming nearer,
the watchman saw another man running;
and he called out to the gatekeeper,
"There is another man running alone."
And the king said, "That one, too, brings news."
The watchman said, "I can see that the first one runs
like Ahimaaz son of Zadok"; to which the king replied,
"He is a good man, and he comes with good news."
Ahimaaz called out and said to the king, "All is well!"

He bowed low with his face to the ground and said,
"Praised be the LORD your God,
who has delivered up the men
who raised their hand against my lord the king."
The king asked, "Is my boy Absalom safe?"
And Ahimaaz answered, "I saw a large crowd
when your servant Joab was sending your servant off,
but I don't know what it was about."
The king said, "Step aside and stand over there";
he stepped aside and waited.
Just then the Cushite came up; and the Cushite said,
"Let my lord the king be informed that the LORD has
vindicated you today against all who rebelled against you!"
The king asked the Cushite, "Is my boy Absalom safe?"
And the Cushite replied,
"May the enemies of my lord the king and all who rose
      against you to do you harm fare like that young man!"

[1]

David awaits news of the battle against Absalom / Mahane Yehuda market
130 x 160 cm   1995

II SAMUEL 19.1
THE KING WAS SHAKEN. HE WENT UP TO THE
UPPER CHAMBER OF THE GATEWAY AND WEPT,
MOANING THESE WORDS AS HE WENT,
MY SON ABSALOM! O MY SON, MY SON ABSALOM
IF ONLY I HAD DIED INSTEAD OF YOU!
O ABSALOM, MY SON, MY SON!"

[1]

"O Absalom, my son, my son!" / Ben Yehuda Street
etching, 100 x 100 cm   1994

II Samuel 19: 2-4
Joab was told that the king was weeping and mourning over Absalom.
And the victory that day was turned into mourning for all the troops,
for that day the troops heard that the king was grieving over his son.
The troops stole into town that day
like troops ashamed after running away in battle.

[1]

"Absalom, my son, my son" / Mamilla below the King David Hotel and next to the new Hilton.

150 x 195 cm   1995

II Samuel 19: 6-8
Joab came to the king in his quarters and said,
"Today you have humiliated all your followers, who this day saved your life,
and the lives of your sons and daughters, and the lives of your wives and concubines,
by showing love for those who hate you and hate for those who love you.
For you have made clear today that the officers and men mean nothing to you.
I am sure that if Absalom were alive today and the rest of us dead,
you would have preferred it. Now arise, come out and placate your followers!
For I swear by the LORD that if you do not come out,
not a single man will remain with you overnight;
and that would be a greater disaster for you
than any disaster that has befallen you from your youth until now."

[1]

The General warns David to cease mourning Absalom / Mahane Yehuda market
100 x 110 cm   1995

II Samuel 19: 9
So the king arose and sat down in the gateway;
and when all the troops were told that the king was sitting in the gateway,
all the troops presented themselves to the king.

[1]

"The King was sitting at the gateway" / Shlomzion Hamalka towards Jaffa Road
100 x 116 cm   1981,1996

"The King was sitting at the gateway" / towards the Old City
89 x 116 cm   1997

"The King was sitting at the gateway" / Jaffa Road before the market
100 x 116 cm   1996

The last words of David:
II Samuel 23: 4

And as the light of the morning,
  when the sun riseth,

A morning without clouds;
When through clear shining after rain,
The tender grass springeth out of the earth.   [2]

"The tender grass springeth out of the earth"
100 x 116 cm   1997

"The tender grass springeth out of the earth"
143 x 143cm   1997

II Samuel 23: 13-17
Once, during the harvest, three of the thirty chiefs went down to David
at the cave of Adullam, while a force of Philistines was encamped
in the Valley of Rephaim.
David was in the stronghold,
and a Philistine garrison was then at Bethlehem.
David felt a craving and said,
"If only I could get a drink of water from the cistern
which is by the gate of Bethlehem!"
So the three warriors got through the Philistine camp
and drew water from the cistern which is by the gate of Bethlehem,
and they carried it back.
But when they brought it to David he would not drink it,
and he poured it out as a libation to the LORD.
For he said, "The LORD forbid that I should do this!
Can I drink the blood of the men who went at the risk of their lives?"
So he would not drink it.
Such were the exploits of the three warriors.

[1]

"If only I could get a drink of water from the cistern which is by the gate of Bethlehem!"
116 x 146 cm   1996

I was raised near this elevated subway station at Mosholu Parkway in the
Bronx, which is very much a stronghold. It borders on Van Cortlandt Park,
where the Philistine's are encamped. I draw David's three warriors after a
1950 photograph by Robert Capa shot in Israel.

II Samuel 24: 1-17

The anger of the LORD again flared up against Israel;
and He incited David against them, saying, "Go and number Israel and Judah."
The king said to Joab, his army commander,
"Make the rounds of all the tribes of Israel, from Dan to Beer-sheba,
and take a census of the people, so that I may know the size of the population."
Joab answered the king, "May the LORD your God increase the number of the people
a hundredfold, while your own eyes see it! But why should my lord king want this?"
However, the king's command to Joab and to the officers of the army remained firm;
and Joab and the officers of the army set out, at the instance of the king,
to take a census of the people of Israel.
They crossed the Jordan and encamped at Aroer, on the right side of the town,
which is in the middle of the wadi of Gad, and went on to Jazer.
They continued to Gilead and to the region of Tahtim-hodshi,
and they came to Dan-jaan and around to- Sidon.
They went onto the fortress of Tyre and all the towns of the Hivites and Canaanites,
and finished at Beer-sheba in southern Judah.
They traversed the whole country,
and then they came back to Jerusalem at the end of nine months and twenty days.
Joab reported to the king the number of the people that had been recorded:
in Israel there were 800,000 soldiers ready to draw the sword,
and the men of Judah numbered 500,000.
But afterward David reproached himself for having numbered the people.
And David said to the LORD, "I have sinned grievously in what I have done.
Please, O LORD, remit the guilt of Your servant, for I have acted foolishly."
When David rose in the morning,
the word of the LORD had come to the prophet Gad, David's seer:
"Go and tell David, 'Thus said the LORD:
I hold three things over you; choose one of them, and I will bring it upon you.'"
Gad came to David and told him; he asked,
"Shall a seven-year famine come upon you in the land,
or shall you be in flight from your adversaries for three months while they pursue you,
or shall there be three days of pestilence in your land?
Now consider carefully what reply I shall take back to Him who sent me."
David said to Gad, "I am in great distress.
Let us fall into the hands of the LORD, for his compassion is great;
and let me not fall into the hands of men."
The LORD sent a pestilence upon Israel from morning until the set time;
and 70,000 of the people died, from Dan to Beer-sheba.
But when the angel extended his hand against Jerusalem to destroy it,
the LORD renounced further punishment and said to the angel
who was destroying the people, "Enough! Stay your hand!"
The angel of the LORD was then by the threshing floor
of Araunah the Jebusite.
When David saw the angel who was striking down the people,
he said to the LORD,
"I alone am guilty, I alone have done wrong;
but these poor sheep,
what have they done?
Let Your hand fall upon me and my father's house!"

The Angel of Death / Ben Yehuda Street
53 x 45 cm   1982

[1]

The Angel of Death / Jaffa Road
135 x 160 cm   1982

II Samuel 24: 18-25

Gad came to David the same day and said to him,
"Go and set up an altar to the LORD on the threshing floor of Araunah the Jebusite."
David went up, following Gad's instructions, as the LORD had commanded.
Araunah looked out and saw the king and his courtiers approaching him.
So Araunah went out and bowed low to the king, with his face to the ground.
And Araunah asked, "Why has my lord the king come to his servant?"
David replied, "To buy the threshing floor from you,
that I may build an altar to the LORD
and that the plague against the people may be checked."
And Araunah said to David, "Let my lord the king take it and offer up whatever he
sees fit. Here are oxen for a burnt offering, and the threshing boards
and the gear of the oxen for wood.
All this, O king, Araunah gives to Your Majesty.
And may the LORD your God," Araunah added, "respond to you with favor!"
But the king replied to Araunah, "No, I will buy them from you at a price.
I cannot sacrifice to the LORD my God burnt offerings that have cost me nothing."
So David bought the threshing floor and the oxen for fifty shekels of silver.
And David built there an altar to the LORD
and sacrificed burnt offerings and offerings of well-being.
The LORD responded to the plea for the land,
and the plague against Israel was checked.   [1]

The threshing floor of Araunah: On mount Moriah, the hill to the east of Jerusalem on which the Temple was afterwards built. The site on which David built his altar is generally accepted as that on which the Temple altar of burnt-offering later stood. It is now occupied by the Dome of the Rock.

David purchases the threshing floor
60 x 61 cm   1974, 1996

David purchases the threshing floor / Judean hill and Ben Yehuda Street
painted etching, 100 x 100 cm   1995

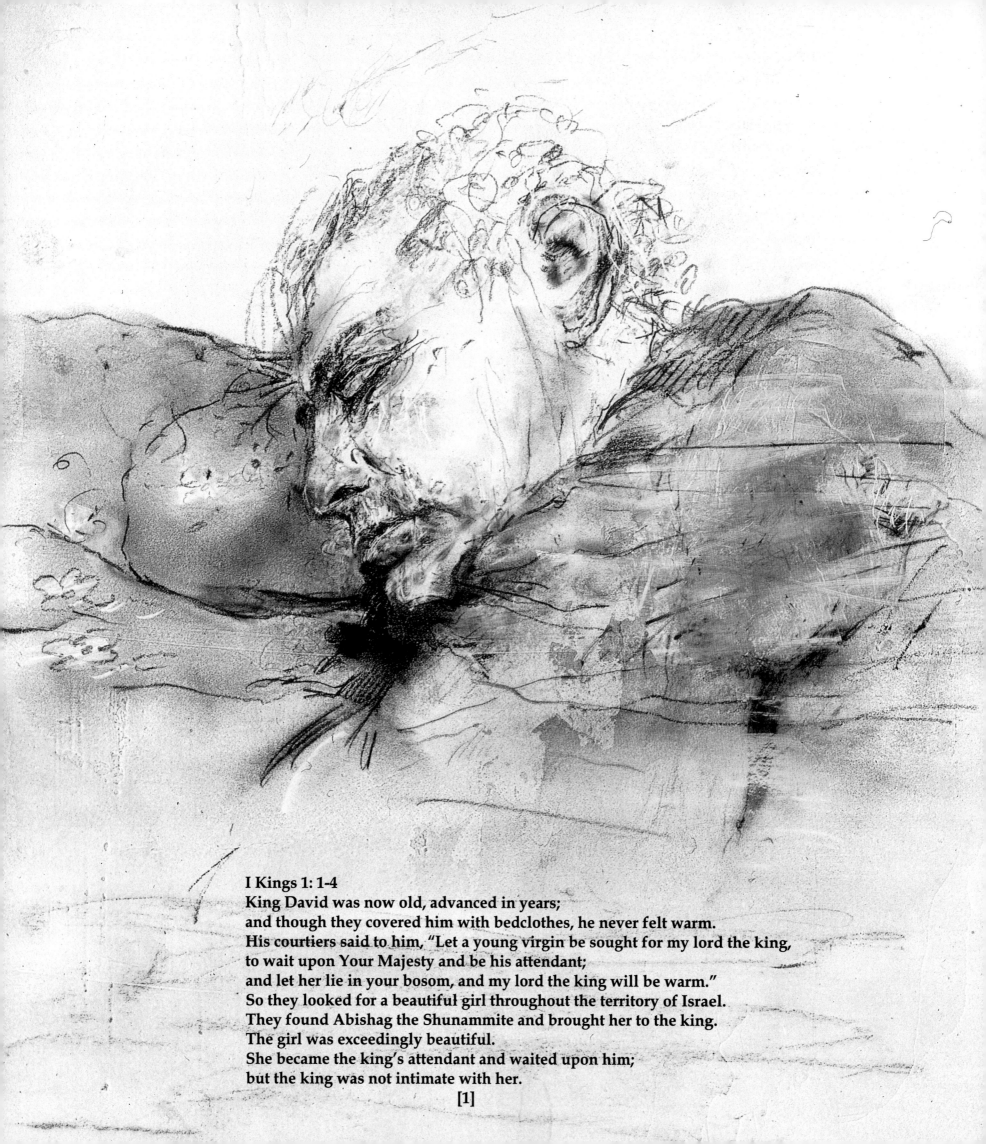

I Kings 1: 1-4
King David was now old, advanced in years;
and though they covered him with bedclothes, he never felt warm.
His courtiers said to him, "Let a young virgin be sought for my lord the king,
to wait upon Your Majesty and be his attendant;
and let her lie in your bosom, and my lord the king will be warm."
So they looked for a beautiful girl throughout the territory of Israel.
They found Abishag the Shunammite and brought her to the king.
The girl was exceedingly beautiful.
She became the king's attendant and waited upon him;
but the king was not intimate with her.

[1]

David and Abishag
130 x 116 cm   1996

153

David and Abishag
etching, same size   1996

This sleeping figure on both pages is recycled from
an earlier work based on Charlie Chaplin's "1 AM".
My muse is gone, simply replaced by the young Abishag.
This is a subject of the future.

David and Abishag / view to Jaffa Road
97 x 114 cm   1995

I Kings 1: 5-14
Now Adonijah son of Haggith went about boasting,
"I will be king!"
He provided himself with chariots and horses,
and an escort of fifty outrunners.
His father had never scolded him:
"Why did you do that?"
He was the one born after Absalom and, like him,
was very handsome.
He conferred with Joab son of Zeruiah
and with the priest Abiathar,
and they supported Adonijah; but the priest Zadok,
Benaiah son of Jehoiada,
the prophet Nathan, Shimei and Rei,
and David's own fighting men
did not side with Adonijah.
Adonijah made a sacrificial feast of sheep, oxen,
and fatlings at the Zoheleth stone
which is near En-rogel;
he invited all his brother princes
and all the king's courtiers of the tribe of Judah;
but he did not invite the prophet Nathan,
or Benaiah, or the fighting men,
or his brother Solomon.
Then Nathan said to Bathsheba, Solomon's mother,
"You must have heard that Adonijah son of Haggith
has assumed the kingship
without the knowledge of our lord David.
Now take my advice,
so that you may save your life
and the life of your son Solomon.
Go immediately to King David and say to him,
'Did not you, O lord king,
swear to your maid-servant;
"Your son Solomon shall succeed me as king,
and he shall sit upon my throne"?
They why has Adonijah become king?'
While you are still there talking with the king,
I will come in after you and confirm your words."
[1]

156

Bronx elevated subway over Judea
52 x 55 cm   1997

Natan's advice to Bat-Sheva / Bronx subway station (Mosholu Parkway)
51 x 59 in   1999

I Kings 1: 15-31

So Bathsheba went to the king in his chamber.

The king was very old,

and Abishag the Shunammite was waiting on the king.

Bathsheba bowed low in homage to the king;

and the king asked, "What troubles you?" She answered him,

"My lord, you yourself swore to your maidservant by the LORD your God:

'Your son Solomon shall succeed me as king, and he shall sit upon my throne.'

Yet now Adonijah has become king, and you, my lord the king,

know nothing about it.

He has prepared a sacrificial feast of a great many oxen, fatlings, and sheep,

and he has invited all the king's sons and Abiathar the priest

and Joab commander of the army; but he has not invited your servant Solomon.

And so the eyes of all Israel are upon you, O lord king,

to tell them who shall succeed my lord the king on the throne.

Otherwise, when my lord the king lies down with his fathers,

my son Solomon and I will be regarded as traitors."

She was still talking to the king when the prophet Nathan arrived.

They announced to the king, "The prophet Nathan is here,"

and he entered the king's presence.

Bowing low to the king with his face to the ground, Nathan said,

"O lord king, you must have said, 'Adonijah shall succeed me as king

and he shall sit upon my throne.'

For he has gone down today and prepared a sacrificial feast

of a great many oxen, fatlings, and sheep.

He invited all the king's sons and the army officers and Abiathar the priest.

At this very moment they are eating and drinking with him,

and they are shouting, 'Long live King Adonijah!'

But he did not invite me your servant,

or the priest Zadok, or Benaiah son of Jehoiada, or your servant Solomon.

Can this decision have come from my lord the king,

without your telling your servant

who is to succeed to the throne of my lord the king?"

King David's response was: "Summon Bathsheba!"

She entered the king's presence and stood before the king.

And the king took an oath saying,

"As the LORD lives, who has rescued me from every trouble:

The oath I swore to you by the LORD, the God of Israel,

that your son Solomon should succeed me as king

and that he should sit upon my throne in my stead,

I will fulfill this very day!"

Bathsheba bowed low in homage to the king with her face to the ground,

and she said, "May my lord King David live forever!"

[1]

Bathsheba appeals to David for Solomon's succession to the throne / outside artist's studio
135 x 143 cm   1995

Artist's Biography

Schwebel was born in West Virginia in 1932 and raised in Georgia until his family moved to the Bronx in 1938, where he attended school. He studied theater for two years with Sanford Meisner at the Neighborhood Playhouse before serving in the U.S. Army in Japan from 1953 to 1955. There he started drawing and working under the Zen master, Kimura Kyoen in Kyoto – a period that had a profound impact on his art.

Returning to New York, Schwebel began six years of study in art history at New York University and the Institute of Fine Arts, painting whenever possible. His efforts were supported by friendships with Rube Kadish, sculptor, and with Philip Guston, who was at that time in the process of rejecting his own abstract expressionism – an important influence in Schwebel's independence.

In 1962, Schwebel left the university to travel in Europe. The following year, on a visit to Israel, he restored a deserted house in Ein Karem on the outskirts of Jerusalem where he and his family have lived ever since. From then on, responding to his environment - whether the Judean hills, Jerusalem, Tel Aviv or New York - has become a major force in his painting. He combines actual modern-day surroundings with extensive personal experience, including drawings done while on an artillery gun in the Yom Kippur War, or paintings of "the Sealed Room" during the Gulf War.

Schwebel has made recurring visits to New York, for his work on *Houdini, the great self-liberator*, who freed himself while hanging upside down over city streets; the three-sewer hitter, the heroic stick-ball player of his youth in the Bronx; and the *Dragon of the Parking Lot*. Dragons have always held a significant position in Schwebel's iconography, and recent paintings about *The Dragon Who Would Be A Sculpture* deal with the artist's view of modern sculpture.

His largest body of work, over two hundred pieces, is on David in the book of Samuel. Here he reflects on the land of Israel, its society and politics. The reflections grow in power as the Bible makes the journey from Jerusalem to New York. His first publication of these early works, *The Arena of Jerusalem*, (Tel Aviv, Modan, 1987), contained paintings linking the situations in the Bible to the war in Lebanon.

Schwebel's interest in environment has led to the free standing painting, a wall or series of walls, painted on both sides, and meant to respond to the locale. Three have been constructed, including one at the Israel Museum and another on his own hillside. In Tel Aviv, he executed four seven-meter murals on the outer walls of the main concert hall. An affair with the city resulted in a book, *Tel Aviv, Tel Aviv*, (Tel Aviv, Modan, 1987). Here movie stars and romance, as for instance, Garbo and Barrymore in *Grand Hotel*, take over the streets. Schwebel's journals, which he has kept for over forty years, reinforce these pages with his work-process and humor.

In the early 90's, Schwebel began work commemorating the Expulsion of the Jews from Spain. His research led him to connect that history with the Holocaust; the paintings and historical documentation are combined in an unpublished book entitled *The Inescapable*.

In 1999, Schwebel achieved critical acclaim with the inclusion of some of his David works as illustrations for *Give Us A King!*, (New York, Schocken Books, 1999), Everett Fox's translation and commentary on the book of Samuel.